A TREASURY OF THE

GREAT OPERAS

BY ARTUR HOLDE

BANTAM BOOKS · TORONTO · NEW YORK · LONDON

A TREASURY OF THE GREAT OPERAS
A Bantam Book / published November 1965

Library of Congress Catalog Card Number: 65-26666

All rights reserved.
Copyright © 1965 by Bantam Books, Inc.
This book may not be reproduced in whole or in part,
by mimeograph or any other means, without
permission in writing from the publisher.

Published simultaneously in the United States and Canada.

Bantam Books are published by Bantam Books, Inc., a subsidiary
of Grosset & Dunlap, Inc. Its trade-mark, consisting of the words
"Bantam Books" and the portrayal of a bantam, is registered in the
United States Patent Office and in other countries. Marca Registrada.
Bantam Books, Inc., 271 Madison Avenue, New York, N.Y. 10016.

PRINTED IN THE UNITED STATES OF AMERICA

TABLE OF CONTENTS

As part of his plan to open the Suez Canal with the greatest possible pomp, the Khedive of Egypt commissioned a work by Giuseppe Verdi (1813-1901). The première, set for 1869, was to coincide with the opening of Cairo's new opera house. Although the plans for the Canal were going smoothly, Verdi's work was behind schedule. Thus, with further delays caused by the Franco-Prussian War, the première did not take place until 1871.

As Verdi could not seem to find an appropriate subject, his friend Camille du Locle tried to interest him in a story of ancient Egypt. Just as the impresario Merelli had subtly brought the *Nabucco* libretto to the composer's attention, so did du Locle set before him *Aïda*. Once again Verdi's imagination caught fire. His dramatic instincts were immediately stimulated by the exotic atmosphere, the tragic finale, and the power of the great ensembles. Du Locle was prepared to elaborate upon the libretto sketches, but Verdi, insisting he be allowed to select his own librettist, chose Antonio Ghislanzoni. By the time the manuscript was delivered, Verdi had already composed the final scene. Stirred

Elena Nikolaidi as Amneris in the Metropolitan Opera's production of the early 1950's. On a terrace in the palace in

beyond patience by his drive to create, he had already set to music what he called his own "horrible verses."

· · ·

Opera in 4 acts. Libretto by Antonio Ghislanzoni, aided by the composer. From the French of Camille du Locle, after a prose sketch by Mariette-Bey. *Première:* Cairo Opera House, 1871.

Characters: King of Egypt (bass); Amneris, his daughter (mezzo-soprano); Aïda, Ethiopian slave (soprano); Radames, captain of the Egyptian guard (tenor); Ramfis, high priest (bass); Amonasro, King of Ethiopia, Aïda's father (baritone); messenger (tenor); priests, priestesses, soldiers, prisoners, Egyptians.

Locale: Memphis and Thebes. *Time:* During the reign of the Pharaohs.

· · ·

Act I. In the palace of the King, Radames learns that the deity has selected a warrior to lead the armies against the

Thebes, a ballet divertissement amuses the princess as she longs for the return of her beloved Radames, while he is in battle.

Ethiopians. He hopes to be the chosen one, so that as victor he may claim the slave-girl Aïda for his heroic deeds. The ruler appears to announce the name of the honored soldier; it is Radames. The latter receives the blessings of the priests in the temple of Vulcan, and the sacred sword is given him ceremoniously. Aïda prays for Radames' victory, even though she knows this will mean misery for her people.

Act II. Amneris, who also loves Radames, wants to learn Aïda's feelings for the hero, and she tells the slave-girl that Radames has died in battle. Aïda's grief is uncontrolled, but when Amneris admits that Radames is really alive, her joy is unbounded. Enraged, Amneris tells Aïda that although they are rivals, her power as princess is greater.

Amid cheers from crowds that have gathered, Radames returns. Aïda catches sight of her father, King Amonasro, among the prisoners. He does not want his identity revealed, and therefore he states that the Ethiopian monarch has perished. Radames, offered the reward of his choice by the Egyptian king, asks only for the freedom of the prisoners. The high priest, however, insists that Aïda and her father remain as hostages. As a further token of his gratitude, the King offers Radames the hand of Amneris. The lament of Aïda and Radames over their thwarted hopes mingles with the exultation of the crowd.

Herbert Graf's spectacular staging of the Triumphal Scene at

Act III. On the banks of the Nile the high priest and Amneris meet on the evening prior to her marriage. Aïda appears for a last rendezvous with Radames. Amonasro, who has followed his daughter, tells her that the Ethiopians are preparing an attack. As a daughter of Ethiopia, it is her duty to learn the path to be taken by the Egyptian army. When Radames enters, Aïda suggests they flee together and, in a state of deep emotional conflict, she persuades Radames to tell the secret. Surprised by Amneris and the high priest, Amonasro and Aïda flee. Amneris accuses Radames of high treason. Radames admits his guilt and hands the guards his sword.

Act IV. Amneris still hopes to win Radames, but her attempts to save him are in vain. The judges condemn him to be entombed alive in the dungeon beneath the temple. Amneris curses her own jealousy, and Radames, who had maintained silence throughout his trial, refuses her offers to intercede with the King.

Sealed in the tomb, Radames awaits his end. Suddenly in the darkness he discovers Aïda. Unobserved, she has slipped into the tomb to perish with him. Radames and Aïda affirm their undying love, and their song unites with the faraway chant of the priests. Meanwhile Amneris, kneeling on the stone that seals the tomb, offers a prayer to Heaven.

the outdoor arena of Verona. The setting is by Piero Zuffi.

The Barber

of Seville

THE BARBER OF SEVILLE

The history of this opera is typical of the conditions under which Italian composers of the eighteenth and nineteenth centuries often were forced to work. At the end of 1815 young Gioacchino Rossini (1792-1868) had made a contract with the owner of the Teatro di Torre Argentina in Rome obliging him to set to music for the forthcoming carnival season any libretto supplied to him. The first half of the score was due by January 20, 1816, and the remainder by the beginning of February. However, various intended libretti were rejected by the censor. A quick decision was made in favor of Beaumarchais' comedy, *Le Barbier de Séville,* even though it had already been set to music repeatedly, most successfully by Giovanni Paisiello. Within twenty days Rossini completed the entire score.

For the strangest reasons, the première turned out to be a fiasco. Though the work, out of consideration for Paisiello's opera, had at first been named *Almaviva; ossia, L'Inutile Precauzione* (Almaviva; or, The Useless Precaution), numerous followers of Paisiello revealed their hostile attitude. A Spanish song with guitar accompaniment was substituted for Almaviva's serenade, but the guitar was out of tune and had to be tuned on the open stage. At his entrance, Basilio fell down, cutting his mouth and nose. As if these mishaps were not enough, a cat turned up on the stage, and the performance ended to the accompaniment of laughter, whistles, and hisses. With stoic indifference, Rossini went home and was fast asleep when friends came to console him. On the following day the composer made some changes, but, to avoid being a direct witness to further disappointment, he did not attend the second performance. The unexpected happened: this time the opera was received with enthusiasm.

Although it attains neither the depth of feeling nor the wealth of musical invention of Mozart's sequel, *Le Nozze di Figaro,* Rossini's opera charms by humor, noble melody, and witty characterization. Figaro's entrance, *Largo al factotum della città* ("Make way for the factotum of the town"), Basilio's aria, "La calumnia," and the "salutation" duet between Dr. Bartolo and Basilio's pretended substitute, demonstrate a true mastery of Italian comedy.

•   •   •

Comic opera in 3 acts. Libretto by Cesare Sterbini, after the play by Pierre Beaumarchais. *Première:* Teatro di

Torre Argentina, Rome, 1816.

Characters: Count Almaviva (tenor); Dr. Bartolo (bass); Rosina, his ward (soprano); Figaro, barber (baritone); Basilio, music master (bass); Fiorello, Almaviva's servant (bass); Berta, Dr. Bartolo's housekeeper (soprano); Ambrogio, Bartolo's servant; sergeant of the guard (tenor or baritone); notary.

Locale: Seville. *Time:* Eighteenth century.

• • •

Act I. Early one morning Count Almaviva, accompanied by a group of musicians, sings a serenade to Rosina, the ward of Dr. Bartolo. Figaro passes by with his guitar, and the Count confides to him his intention of marrying Rosina. He expects good advice from Figaro, who enjoys some renown for his inventiveness in matters of love. While they are talking, Rosina appears on the balcony and, discovering her admirer, wants to give him a letter; but Bartolo, having followed her to the balcony, asks her what paper she holds in her hand. She answers that it is the text of an aria from the new opera, *L'Inutile Precauzione,* then lets the paper drop as if by accident. While Bartolo runs down to retrieve it, the Count quickly picks it up and hides. In her note Rosina asks her unknown admirer to find some means of letting her know his name, station, and intentions. Figaro then gives his guitar to the Count and advises him to explain everything in another song. Not wanting to reveal his identity, he tells her that his name is Lindoro, that he is not rich, but loves her dearly and wants to marry her.

Now the problem is how to get into the house. Oh, that is simple, says Figaro. Disguised as a soldier, the Count is to present a billeting order to Dr. Bartolo, pretending to be a member of a regiment expected in Seville that very day.

Act II. Rosina is disconsolate because Bartolo, who wants to marry her for her considerable fortune, keeps her in complete isolation. Rosina's singing teacher, Basilio, informs Bartolo that a certain Count Almaviva is pursuing his ward, and he advises him to get rid of the Count by spreading slander. Figaro has overheard this conversation and warns Rosina. By various explanations, she allays Bartolo's suspicions that she is secretly writing letters to strangers. Actually she had written a few lines to "Lindoro" and given them to Figaro for delivery.

Now the Count, disguised as a soldier and seemingly drunk, arrives. Bartolo refuses to admit the unwanted guest, since, as a doctor, he is exempt from having soldiers billeted upon him. During the argument the Count whispers to Rosina, "I am Lindoro," drops a note to the floor, then hands it to her, but not without arousing Bartolo's suspicion. Having made a quick substitution, she explains that the paper is only the laundry list, and when he tears it from her hand, it is exactly that; Bartolo has again been fooled. The Count, overplaying his part of the drunken soldier, quarrels with Bartolo. The guard is alerted, "Lindoro" shows the sergeant a paper, and the guard immediately retires, to the stunned surprise of all present.

Act. III. Since the billeting scheme misfired, Almaviva now has a new plan. In clerical dress, he arrives at Bartolo's house to give Rosina her music lesson, substituting for Don Basilio, who supposedly is ill. Distrusting this "Don Alonzo," Dr. Bartolo remains in the room to be shaved right there by Figaro. Suddenly Basilio appears, obviously in the best of health. Almaviva saves the embarrassing situation by quietly slipping Basilio a well-filled purse. Now it is easy to convince him that he suffers from a high fever and should go to bed at once.

Salvatore Baccaloni as Doctor Bartolo and Lily Pons as Rosina in a Metropolitan Opera Company's production of the 1940's.

The "music lesson" is resumed, while Figaro does his best to distract Bartolo's attention. But when Bartolo overhears the Count's remark about a disguise, he at once suspects a new conspiracy and goes into a wild rage. Rosina withdraws to her room. Figaro and the Count leave. Then Bartolo sends for Don Basilio, who tells him he does not know "Don Alonzo" and that, in fact, he is almost certain that he is Count Almaviva. Now Basilio is to bring the notary over to the house at once. Bartolo tells Rosina that "Don Alonzo" and Figaro have conspired to win her affection only to hand her over to Count Almaviva. Furious, she consents to marry her guardian. Bartolo leaves to make final preparations for the wedding.

A thunderstorm breaks. As it subsides, Almaviva and Figaro climb a ladder and enter the room, intending to abduct Rosina as planned. Much to their surprise, Rosina refuses, accusing "Lindoro" of treachery. The Count then reveals his true identity, and Rosina happily consents.

Before the abduction can be carried out Bartolo returns with the notary. The latter, having already been instructed by Figaro, legalizes the marriage contract between the Count and Rosina. There is nothing left for him to do but to make the best of it. As a consolation, the Count waives all claims to Rosina's dowry.

The jealous Doctor Bartolo watches suspiciously as Count Almaviva, in disguise (center) pays his respects to Rosina.

La

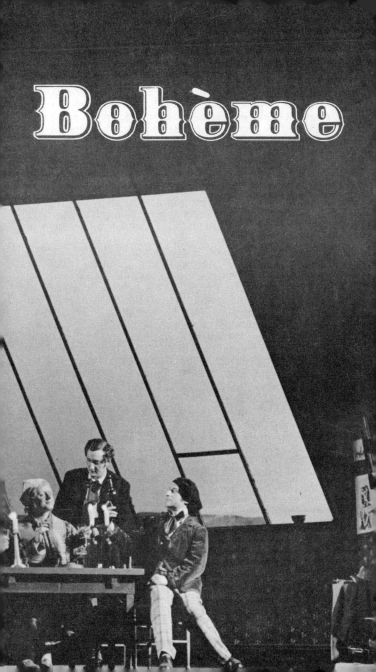

Bohème

LA BOHÈME

Giacomo Puccini (1858-1924) belongs among the few great composers who, along with Richard Strauss, have enriched the art of opera after Wagner and Verdi. From the turn of the century until today, *La Bohème, Tosca,* and *Madama Butterfly* have been pillars in the repertoire of every operatic enterprise. Such popularity is not to be explained by any wave of fashion, by any vigorous performance or distinguished interpretation, but only by music of masterful force, based on three exceptional librettos. Puccini's librettists, Giacosa and Illica, inspired by Murger, Sardou, and Belasco, and closely following the intentions of the composer in all three operas, were able to produce a logical and exciting action. They also fulfilled the demands of the musician by providing aria forms, large ensembles, and finales made up of unusual combinations of the characters.

On his father's side, Puccini was descended from a family of musicians who had been living in Lucca for many generations. Upon completing his studies at the Milan Conservatory, Puccini set his sights on opera. After his moderately successful first work, the composer attracted much attention with *Manon Lescaut.* Three years later the breakthrough came with *La Bohème.* The pattern of success was followed by both *Tosca* and *Madama Butterfly,* but *La Fanciulla del West* (The Girl of the Golden West), first presented at the Metropolitan Opera in New York, was not well received. Dramatic masterpieces followed at equal intervals, among them the sprightly, somewhat cynical *Gianni Schicchi,* a one-act comedy about the probation of a will, and *Turandot,* an unfinished opera in three acts whose last scene was completed by Franco Alfano, based on the sketches by Puccini.

Puccini's fame rests on many qualities: he was a melodist who handled vocal line masterfully; he painted the dramatic setting with extremely characteristic, penetrating colors; but above all, as a sensitive observer of the intimate moods of the soul, he created a very personal musical style that did complete justice to the psychological contents of the librettos and at the same time spiritualized the pervading, powerful erotic element.

•　　　•　　　•

Opera in 4 acts. Libretto by Giuseppe Giacosa and Luigi Illica, based on Henri Murger's book, *La Vie de Bohème.*

Première: Teatro Reggio, Turin, 1896.

Characters: Marcello, painter (baritone); Rodolfo, poet (tenor); Schaunard, musician (baritone); Colline, philosopher (bass); Benoit, landlord (bass); Mimi, seamstress (soprano); Musetta, girl of the Latin Quarter (soprano); Parpignol, vendor of toys (tenor); Alcindoro, admirer of Musetta (bass); customs guard (bass).

Locale: Paris. *Time:* About 1830.

•   •   •

Act I. On a cold Christmas day Marcello sits working in front of his easel in his unheated garret, while his friend Rodolfo gazes thoughtfully out the window. Marcello wants to use a stool for fuel; Rodolfo, however, tears up one of his plays and throws it, act by act, onto the flames. Colline appears with an armful of books. He is angry because the pawnshop is closed. Then Schaunard appears, bringing wine and firewood; a new piano pupil has just paid him for the first lesson. The general rejoicing is interrupted by the landlord, Benoit, who wants to collect the rent. After some wine has loosened his tongue, he describes his adventures in love. The four bohemians pretend to be shocked and push him out the door, naturally without having paid a sou of the rent.

Rodolfo has to write an article and asks his friends to leave him alone for a while. But he is not in the right mood for the article. There is a knock on the door: a young girl stands outside. Her candle has gone out. Rodolfo asks her in to sit down, since she is exhausted from climbing the stairs. He notices sympathetically her beautiful but pale face. She leaves with her relit candle, but soon returns, for during their conversation she had dropped her key. The candle is snuffed again by a draft, and during their search for the key in the dark they find each other's hands and hearts. Rodolfo tells her about himself, and Mimi describes her life: her work, her poverty, her struggles. The two lovers have each found in the other an understanding soul. Rodolfo's friends call impatiently from the street. He invites Mimi to go with him to the Café Momus, where he is to meet the others. She accepts, and arm in arm they leave the atelier.

Act II. The gayest Christmas mood prevails in the Latin Quarter. Citizens, soldiers, women, and children are outside the Café Momus. Wares and sweetmeats are on sale. The friends sit at a table in front of the café. They order a sumptuous meal. Marcello is depressed because a group has sat down at a neighboring table and among them he sees his former beloved, Musetta, with an old coxcomb. Musetta tries to win Marcello back by singing a provocative, frivolous waltz song, in which everyone joins. She leaves with her companions to follow a parade of the changing of the guard. Her suitor, Alcindoro, is left behind and, with the greatest displeasure, finds he must pay the check for the entire company.

Act III. A cold, mournful winter morning by the toll gate in a suburb of Paris. There is an inn there, on a small square, in which Marcello and Musetta have settled. They quarrel continually. Rodolfo has sought them out, in order to tell his friends about his disagreements with Mimi, who also appears and, outside the inn, describes to Marcello Rodolfo's groundless jealousy. She quickly hides as Rodolfo comes out of the inn, and overhears him say that he believes she is terribly ill and he has only an unheated room to offer her. He feels they should separate, though he loves her dearly. When Mimi steps out of her hiding place, Marcello leaves the two alone. A touching parting scene follows, full of memories of the happy hours of their life

A scene from Act One, as presented by the NBC TV Opera Theater. Left to right: Colline, Schaunard, Rodolfo and Marcello, a rowdy quartet of happy-go-lucky Bohemians.

together. She feels that their inner union has not ended and resolves not to part until the beginning of spring. Their conversation is interrupted by a quarrel between Marcello and Musetta. The impolitely ironic words accompanying that breakup alternate with the sad, loving phrases with which Rodolfo and Mimi foresee the end of their life together.

Act IV. The scene is again Marcello's garret. Rodolfo is working on a manuscript while Marcello paints. Neither of them can concentrate, for they cannot keep their minds off their abandoned loved ones. When Schaunard and Colline appear with bread and a herring, their spirits are quickly revived. They begin to dance merrily and feign a duel. Suddenly all happiness ends: Musetta brings in Mimi, sick and dying. She wants to be near her beloved and is put to bed on the couch. Musetta gives her expensive earrings to Marcello to pawn to pay for a doctor and medicine. Colline takes his old coat, which he also intends to pledge. The friends leave Mimi and Rodolfo alone. As she thinks about the happy time of their young love, she feels new strength. She falls asleep; the friends return. Standing at the foot of the bed, Schaunard notices that her breathing has stopped. "She is dead," he whispers to Marcello. Rodolfo, in tears, falls upon the dead girl.

Musetta sings her famous Waltz Song in Act Two of the NBC TV production. Marcello (center) is obviously more interested in it than are his carefree Bohemian friends.

Boris

It was not until more than two decades after his death that the works of Modest Petrovitch Moussorgsky (1835-1881) began to gain recognition on an international scale. For a long time many judged him "an amateur of genius." Even Russian contemporaries such as Balakirev, Rimsky-Korsakov and Borodin, while recognizing his great talent, emphasized the discrepancy between his musical inspiration and the realization of his intentions.

Moussorgsky came from a family that loved and understood music. His highly talented mother gave him his first piano lessons, and his father was seriously concerned about his further musical training. When Modest, only ten years old, left the parental estate to continue his education in St. Petersburg, his father engaged a renowned pianist as his teacher. But after two years of this training the boy was sent to a military school, and there was no possibility that he could have acquired a sufficient theoretical basis for composition. The lessons he later received from Balakirev consisted merely of a quasi-improvised playing of the student's compositions, thus Moussorgsky had to leave a number of large-scale projects in the planning stage. Then, when the abolition of serfdom caused the family fortune to decline, the young composer was forced to accept a subordinate position in government service.

Almost to the end of his life Moussorgsky remained in his civil service job. It permitted creative work only on Sundays and holidays. When his mother died in 1865 the young man, already prone to nervous disturbances, began to drink. In spite of his uncontrollable craving, and the interruptions caused by his physical and mental condition, he managed, within the following five years, to complete the work that placed him among the great composers of the nineteenth century.

As in previous cases, Moussorgsky did not simply take over an existing drama. He asked his close friend, the musicologist Vladimir Stassov, to explain the exact details of the historical events that form the basis of Pushkin's play. With Stassov, he dug up library collections of ancient Russian songs and inserted them in the text. Thus, Varlaam's song, "Once upon a time in the city of Kazan," the great chorus of the crowd, "Glory to Russia, glory to Tsar Boris," and the grandiose choral scene at the coronation are derived from early Russian folklore.

When the work was submitted to the Petersburg Imperial Theatre, it was at first rejected. There was no understanding for music that far exceeded conventional bounds and for a libretto representing in the characterizations an absolutely new kind of treatment of historical material. Three years later the theater decided to present a few scenes. In 1874 the same theater gave a complete performance, with moderate success.

Boris Godunov is now one of the most treasured works in opera repertoire. Many scenes, such as the overwhelming coronation scene, the humorous episode of the mendicant friars at the inn, the moving monologue of Boris tormented by his conscience, the Polonaise of the guests, the dialogue of Marina and Dimitry, the unbridled outbreaks of the populace, the breakdown of the Tsar, are musical and dramatic highlights that have never been surpassed in modern operatic literature.

Rimsky-Korsakov sought to give more life to the rather colorless original instrumentation. At present the Metropolitan Opera in New York, as well as other opera houses, prefers the orchestration of Dimitri Shostakovitch, which very effectively stresses the specific Russian character of the music and the mysticism of the mass scenes.

• • •

Opera in 4 acts. Libretto by the composer, based on the drama of the same name by Alexander Pushkin. *Première:* Marinsky Theater, St. Petersburg, 1874.

Characters: Boris Godunov (bass); Fyodor, his son (mezzo-soprano); Xenia, his daughter (soprano); Prince Shuisky, royal councilor (tenor); Andrej Shchelkalov, secretary of the Duma (baritone); Pimen, monk (bass); Gregory (later Dimitry, the Pretender), (tenor); Varlaam (bass); Missail (tenor) and mendicant friars; hostess of the inn (mezzo-soprano); Marina Mnichek, Polish noblewoman (mezzo-soprano); Rangoni, Jesuit priest (bass); Krushov, boyar (tenor); nurse (contralto); The Simpleton (tenor); Lovitsky (tenor) and Chernikofsky (baritone); Jesuit priests; captain of the border guard, guards, soldiers, Polish ladies and gentlemen.

Locale: Russia and Poland. *Time:* 1598-1605.

• • •

Act I, scene 1. Dimitry, the young son of Tsar Ivan the Terrible, has died suddenly under mysterious circumstances. Since there is no direct heir to the crown, a successor has to be chosen. Boris Godunov, who had been appointed Regent for the young son, covets the crown. But he wants to create the impression that he would accept it only upon the urgent demand of the people. He retires to the Monastery of Novodievichy near Moscow, and ruthless policemen assemble a crowd demanding his coronation. Pilgrims, too, chanting devoutly, join the masses. Boris finally gives in to the public clamor.

Scene 2. The coronation is held in the cathedral of the Kremlin. In front of the church a colorful procession takes place while the enthusiastic masses sing an ecstatic hymn. Boris appears in splendid coronation robes, accompanied by his daughter Xenia and his son Fyodor. In this very moment of greatest triumph he feels strong pangs of conscience. He knows that through his connivance ruthless hands murdered the lawful heir.

Scene 3. In Chudov Monastery the old monk Pimen writes the history of Russia while the novice, Gregory, is sleeping. The latter awakes and tells Pimen his strange dreams. Pimen informs him that his chronicle will end with the removal of the Tsarevitch by murderers hired by Boris. This revelation deeply impresses the young monk. He is the same age as the murdered heir, and he resolves to seize the throne.

Scene 4. Two escaped mendicant friars, Varlaam and Missail, enter an inn near the Lithuanian border. While they are drinking and singing, Gregory, who has joined them, asks the innkeeper for the nearest way across the

The famous Inn Scene in Act I at the Metropolitan Opera. Varlaam has had too much to drink, but he tries to read the

border. He plans to raise an army against Boris in Lithuania under the pretext of being Dimitry, the lawful heir to the throne. Suddenly, border police turn up in search of a fugitive monk. The illiterate captain orders Gregory to read the warrant. Gregory changes the words so that the description of the wanted man fits Varlaam. Upon reading the document, however, the falsely denounced man uncovers the fraud. Gregory escapes hurriedly through the window.

Act II, scene 1. The two children of Tsar Boris and their nurse are sitting in a room in the Kremlin. Xenia's thoughts are occupied with her late fiancé. Fyodor studies the map of Russia. To cheer up the girl, the nurse sings a merry song. The Tsar, entering, urges his daughter to forget her sorrow and to seek the companionship of girls her own age. Xenia and the nurse leave the room, and Boris tells his son of the heavy burdens borne by a ruler. A boyar announces Prince Shuisky, who reports a Polish conspiracy against the Tsar. Upon hearing this news, Boris is again seized by his guilty conscience. He demands of Shuisky a detailed report on the murder of the heir to the throne. Maliciously eager for the Tsar's humiliation, Shuisky renders his report with cruel realism. Boris remains alone, deeply stirred. The chimes of the clock strike. Tormented by hallucinations, Boris sees the murdered child

warrant for Dimitry's arrest. As he reads with great effort, he is flanked by his companion, Missail and the suspicious innkeeper.

before him. Sinking into a chair, he begs God for mercy.

Scene 2. In the castle of Sandomir, Marina, the daughter of the wealthy Polish landowner, Mnichek, accepts the homage of her girl friends. But she does not want to hear their sentimental songs; she has fallen in love with the young nobleman, Dimitry, just arrived from Moscow, who is actually Gregory in disguise. With boundless ambition, Marina dreams of mounting the throne of Russia at his side if the plan to overpower Boris should succeed. These ideas are encouraged by the Jesuit priest, Rangoni, who expects the church thereby to gain advantages. She must realize her objective, he advises her, by means of her beauty. In the castle garden Dimitry is waiting for Marina. Rangoni appears, to offer advice and help. Marina, too, comes with many friends. Later she returns alone to assure Dimitry of her love. This scene is overheard by Rangoni in hiding. He exults over the course of events.

Act III, scene 1. The peasants in revolt assemble in the forest of Kromy, near Moscow. They drag in the nobleman Krushov, and mock and mistreat him. They are distracted by the appearance of a poor simpleton who, robbed of his few coins, sings a sad song to himself. The mendicant friars, Varlaam and Missail, arrive as vanguard of Dimitry to stir up the people against Boris. Soon the usurper, Dimitry, appears with his following. He appeals to the populace for support in the struggle against the present ruler. All follow him enthusiastically. Only the simpleton remains behind, and in a melancholy singsong bewails the poor misguided Russian people.

Scene 2. In the great assembly hall of the Kremlin the boyars discuss the possibility of defeating the false Dimitry, who is a threat to all of them. Prince Shuisky, who attends the session, reports on the Tsar's poor state of health. He is obviously haunted by hallucinations. To the surprise of those present, Boris cannot resist the temptation to be present at this secret session. With the consent of the boyars, the monk Pimen, introduced by Shuisky, reports a strange historic event: In a dream a blind man was asked by the murdered heir to pray at his grave for his salvation. The blind man carried out this wish and suddenly regained his sight. Boris cries out in horror and sends for his son Fyodor. The latter is exhorted by his father to rule over his people with justice. He himself will live out his life in a monastery. Overcome by excitement, he falls from the throne and dies.

Giorgio Tozzi as Boris in the NBC TV production attacks the wily Shuisky (Andrew McKinley) in a wild moment of frenzy.

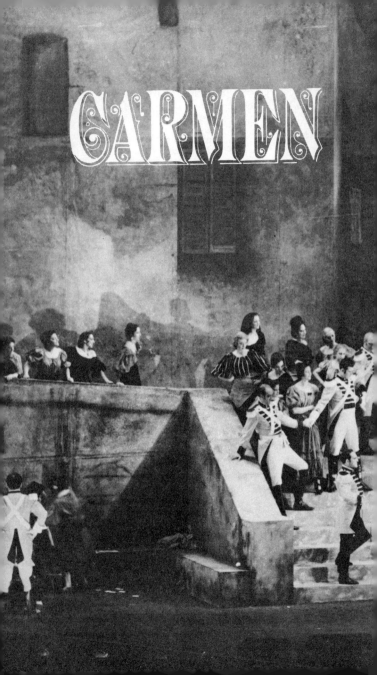

If an attempt were made to determine the half-dozen most popular operas of world literature, it is highly probable that *Carmen* would be among them. Here we have the happy combination of a touching subject, an exceptionally skillful arrangement for the stage, and dramatically effective music of great melodic, rhythmic, and harmonic power. Georges Bizet (1838-1875) never set foot on Spanish soil and, judged from the point of view of folklore, there is nothing authentically Spanish in *Carmen*. Yet the environment, the characterizations, and the color of the music are so striking that scarcely anyone will sense a discrepancy between reality and operatic fantasy.

At its first performance, *Carmen* was not a success. The action was too realistic for the romantic tastes of the public at the Opéra Comique. But the assumption that the composer's death, three months later, was caused by this failure has been disproved. Bizet actually fell victim to pneumonia. Some years later, the composer Ernest Guiraud replaced all the spoken dialogue with recitatives of great sensibility.

• • •

Opera in 4 acts. Libretto by Henri Meilhac and Ludovic Halévy after a novel by Prosper Mérimée. *Première:* Opéra

Carmen (Jean Madeira) taunts her captors while her colleagues from the cigaret factory look on. Vienna State Opera.

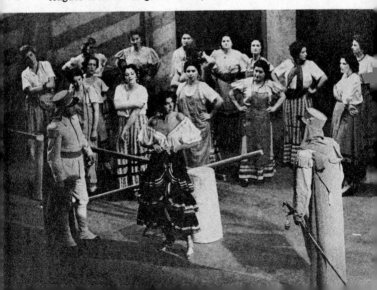

Comique, Paris, 1875.

Characters: Don José, sergeant (tenor); Zuniga, lieutenant (bass); Morales, sergeant (baritone); Escamillo, toreador (baritone); Carmen, gypsy (mezzo-soprano); Micaela, peasant girl (soprano); Frasquita (soprano) and Mercedes (mezzo-soprano), gypsies; Dancairo (tenor) and Remendado (baritone), smugglers.

Locale: In and near Seville. *Time:* About 1820.

· · ·

Act I. The soldiers are watching the crowds passing by. Micaela appears with money and a letter for Don José from his mother. Told that he will come in time for the changing of the guard, she decides to return a little later. Accompanied by street urchins, the new guard marches in. The bell rings in the cigarette factory announcing the noon-time break, and the working girls crowd into the street. One of them is Carmen, a beautiful young gypsy. She tries to attract the attention of Don José by singing the *Habanera*. When he remains indifferent, she throws a flower in his face. The girls are called back to work and Don José picks up the flower pensively. Then Micaela appears, and he feels the strong ties of his distant home. He tells her that the answer to his mother's letter is that he will return

Carmen and her companions gaily entertain themselves at the gypsy camp in the mountains. Metropolitan Opera production.

and marry Micaela. Suddenly the girls rush wildly from the factory and accuse Carmen of having stabbed another girl. Her arms are bound, and she is handed over to Don José's charge. By now she has worked her charm on him, and in the song, *Seguidilla,* Carmen promises that she will meet him in the tavern of Lillas Pastia at the city wall. Sent stumbling by a sudden push from Carmen, Don José lets her escape. He is arrested for his carelessness.

Act II. At the tavern the gypsy girls drink and dance with citizens and soldiers, among them Zuniga and Morales. Zuniga informs Carmen that Don José has been released. Outside jubilant voices are heard, and the famous toreador Escamillo appears with his admirers. He tells of his latest triumphs, but Carmen rejects his advances, for she is waiting for Don José. After the guests have left the tavern, the smugglers venture forth from their hideout. They plan to use the girls to distract the border guards. This time Carmen declines to participate. Her patience is rewarded: Don José arrives and declares his love. She suggests that they escape together, but he refuses to desert his regiment. After engaging in a brawl with Zuniga, however, he finds it impossible to return. No choice is left him but to join the cause of the smugglers.

Act III. The smugglers are resting in the mountains. Don José, whose native village is nearby, is seized by home-sickness. Carmen, whose passion for him has cooled, is fortune-telling with the other girls. For her the cards predict, again and again, one fate—death. Micaela, who has found out Don José's whereabouts, tries to win him back. Escamillo also appears. Don José feels insulted by the toreador's arrogant words. A fight with knives results, but Carmen intervenes to calm them. Escamillo invites them all to a bullfight in Seville in which he will participate. Don José leaves with Micaela when Carmen tells him cynically that he is not suited to the occupation of a smuggler.

Act IV. The crowd gathers as Escamillo arrives arm in arm with Carmen. They declare their mutual love. After the toreador has entered the arena, Frasquita and Mercedes warn Carmen of Don José. But Carmen is not afraid; she will talk to him. In the arena the fight has begun, and Carmen wants to go to her seat when Don José bars her way and implores her to start a new life with him. She rejects his pleas, and he plunges a knife into her breast. She dies, and Don José throws himself over her body.

The celebrated smugglers' quintet of Act Two at the Metropolitan Opera. Left to right: Frasquita (Lucine Amara), Mercedes (Margaret Roggero), Remendado (Alessio DePaolis), Dancairo (George Cehanovsky), and Carmen (Risë Stevens)

Cavalleria Rusticana

From an artistic as well as a human point of view, the life of Pietro Mascagni (1863-1945) did not run a very happy course. As a young musician, he enjoyed the patronage of Count Florestan de Lardarel, and, after the performance of a symphony and choral work, a rapid rise was expected of him. Disappointed after some unimportant engagements with small touring opera companies, he retired from the operatic stage to become musical director of the modest concert activities in Cerignola (Apulia). A competition for a one-act opera caused him to compose *Cavalleria Rusticana*. After the sensational success of the first performance, the work attained international recognition, because of the popular appeal of the melodious music and perhaps even more because of the dramatically effective libretto. Mascagni's other fourteen operas, among them *L'Amico Fritz* (1891) and *Iris* (1905), met with little success. With the rise of fascism in Italy, the composer, who had joined the movement wholeheartedly, expected to usher in a new and more hopeful artistic era for himself. He paid homage to Mussolini in an opera, *Nero*. After the fall of the dictator, Mascagni's considerable fortune was confiscated and he himself was excluded from the public life of Italy. Mascagni died, almost forgotten, in a shabby hotel room in Rome.

• • •

Opera in 1 act. Libretto by Giovanni Targioni-Tozzetti and Guido Menasci, based on a play by Giovanni Verga. *Première:* Teatro Costanzi, Rome, 1890.

Characters: Santuzza, young countrywoman (soprano); Turiddu, young peasant (tenor); Lucia, his mother (contralto); Alfio, teamster (baritone); Lola, Alfio's wife (mezzo-soprano).

Locale: A Sicilian village. *Time:* Nineteenth century.

• • •

During the orchestral Prelude, and with the curtain still closed, Turiddu is heard singing. When the curtain opens, the villagers are seen going to early Mass in the church on the square. Santuzza, who is in love with Turiddu, asks his mother where her son is. She answers that he went to Francofonte to buy wine. Santuzza, however, thinks she saw him in the village the evening before. The teamster, Alfio, returns from a trip. He suspects Turiddu of having resumed a love affair with his wife, Lola. Full of jealousy, Santuzza confronts Turiddu in the church square while the devout are singing the Easter hymn, *Regina coeli*. She demands to know where he spent the night, but he refuses to answer. When she insists, he flings her down brutally on the steps of the church and leaves. In boundless fury she calls after Turiddu: "A bloody Easter for you." When Alfio comes along, Santuzza tells him that Turiddu is his wife's lover. Alfio vows revenge.

Now aware of the hatred she has sown, Santuzza finds herself overcome by remorse. But she is powerless to stop Alfio who, in a rage, has vowed to slay Turiddu. As the carter goes off, Santuzza, torn by guilt, follows Alfio to calm him.

The stage remains empty for a time. During this period the orchestra plays the *Intermezzo sinfonico,* which depicts the Easter peace of the village. The devout leave the church, and Turiddu, accompanied by Lola, invites everybody for a drink in the tavern on the square. Alfio, who has joined the group, brusquely refuses the glass offered him by Turiddu. The women, sensing impending trouble, leave hurriedly with Lola. Only the men remain. Alfio and Turiddu embrace as the prelude to a fight to the death. Turiddu has a guilty conscience, and he shows his readiness to accept Alfio's challenge by biting his ear (an old Sicilian custom). Alfio proceeds to the field of battle, followed by his opponent. Suddenly, a village girl rushes in crying that Alfio has killed Turiddu, and Santuzza falls.

Giuseppe di Stefano as Turiddu drinks his last toast and sings the Drinking Song in the production of La Scala, Milan, 1954.

THE

CONSUL

THE CONSUL

Gian Carlo Menotti (born 1911) emigrated to the United States at the age of seventeen, after five years of study at the Milan Conservatory. Recognizing his unusual talent, the Curtis Institute of Music in Philadelphia accepted him immediately. To the present day he has maintained his Italian citizenship. Perhaps this legal affiliation reflects a deep inner significance for Menotti; as a creating musician he has remained typically Italian. The vital melodic line, gracefully vocal in character, is and has always been an important element in his tonal language. Unlike many of his contemporaries, Menotti has not devoted himself to atonality or the twelve-tone technique. Even though he is unmistakably a man of his time, the composer finds his musical roots in the expressionistic means of Puccini. His versatility is proved by the fact that he writes his own librettos, and in numerous productions has assumed successfully the duties of stage director.

Following the favorable reception of his one-act comedy, *Amelia Goes to the Ball* (1937), Menotti was commissioned by the National Broadcasting Company to write the satirical *Old Maid and the Thief*. It proved a hit, and has been repeated on countless stages. The musical tragedy *The Medium* depicts in stark episodes the manipulations of a deceiving fortune-teller. Up to now, the high point of the composer's output has been *The Consul*, written in 1950. With sympathy and understanding for the victims of the horrible years of oppression and displacement in Europe, Menotti describes here the fate of a family forced from one country to another. The sharply accented music, embracing symbolic as well as realistic devices, is as overpowering as the credible drama it accompanies. The opera secured for Menotti an international reputation. Four years later, he followed this with *The Saint of Bleecker Street*, which treats the lives of Italians in New York City.

Menotti gained a tremendous success with his tenderly lyric *Amahl and the Night Visitors*, which is frequently presented at Christmastime. A recent work is *Maria Golovin*, whose tragic subject once again reflects the dangerous chaos of our times. Menotti's newest operas are *Labyrinth*, a television opera commissioned by NBC, and the comic opera, *The Last Savage*.

• • •

Music drama in 3 acts. Libretto by the composer. *Première:* Shubert Theater, Philadelphia, 1950. Ethel Barrymore Theater, New York, 1950.

45

Characters: John Sorel (baritone); Magda, his wife (soprano); his mother (contralto); agent of the Secret Police (bass); secretary (mezzo-soprano); Mr. Kofner (bassbaritone); Italian woman (soprano); Anna Gomez (soprano); Vera Boronel (alto); Nika Magadoff, magician (tenor); Assan (baritone); two detectives.

Locale: Somewhere in Europe. *Time:* The present.

•   •   •

Act I, scene 1. John Sorel, a fighter in the resistance movement, stumbles wounded into his apartment. He has just barely escaped the Razzia at a meeting with his comrades. His wife and mother hide him, and when he is followed by the police Magda tells the officials that she has not seen her husband for two weeks. Coming out of hiding, John prepares for his immediate flight. He advises his wife to go to the Consul for help. When a stone breaks her window, she will know that the window-repair man Assan is to bring news from him.

Scene 2. A group of visa applicants in the consulate waiting room receive only mechanical attention from the unemotional secretary. Magda begs for permission to speak to the Consul personally concerning her plight. The secre-

The Waiting Room scene in the New York City Opera production where Magda (Patricia Neway) gives way to her tensions.

tary tells her that the Consul is much too busy. She is made to fill out the customary forms and told to return the following week.

Act II, scene 1. No news has come from John. Magda's baby has fallen sick, and she slumps exhausted at the table. She dreams of John, then awakes with a cry. A stone breaks through the window. Magda calls the repair man, who tells her that John is on his way home. Suddenly a detective appears and tries to force Magda into betraying her husband and his cause. Assan tells her that John does not want to cross the border until Magda has received her visa. As the repair man is about to leave the apartment, Magda and her mother-in-law discover that the baby has died.

Scene 2. Magda returns to the consulate. The magician Magadoff demonstrates his bag of tricks, hoping to get a working permit. Eventually, he hypnotizes all those present; they begin to pair off and dance. His case taken care of, the secretary coldly addresses herself to the next one. She tells Magda that she must wait a long time. Strongly aroused, Magda expresses her contempt for a heartless bureaucracy that robs everyone of his inherent dignity. Magda sees the familiar figure of the Secret Police agent leaving the Consul's office, and falls in a faint.

Act III, scene 1. Magda is waiting at the consulate once again. Assan arrives to tell her that John is about to come back; he has learned of the death of his child and the death of his mother that followed soon thereafter. She scribbles a note to warn John of the uselessness of his return. The waiting room has emptied, and Magda leaves, desperate. No sooner has she gone than John bursts in, asking to see his wife. She has already left, the secretary tells him, and continues preparing herself for her date. Hearing voices in the hall, John reaches for his revolver. The Secret Police agent takes away his weapon. Since he cannot arrest John in the neutral territory of the consulate, the detective insists that he leave voluntarily. John agrees, requesting only that he may telephone his wife from the main police station.

Scene 2. The telephone rings in the empty Sorel apartment. Like a sleepwalker, Magda enters the room, too late to hear the phone. She sits down before the gas stove and covers her head with a shawl. She turns on the gas. Her husband, his mother, and figures from the consulate waiting room appear before her as in a dream. The magician speaks to her in hypnotic tones: "You are tired. You want to sleep. Breathe deeply." As Magda collapses forward, the telephone rings again and again.

The secretary (Regina Sarfaty) listens coldly and unsympathetically to the problems of Magda Sorel (Patricia Neway).

COSI

FAN TUTTE

COSÌ FAN TUTTE

The great success of a *Le Nozze di Figaro* revival in Vienna served to renew Kaiser Josef II's interest in Wolfgang Amadeus Mozart (1756-1791). According to legend, it was the monarch himself who gave the composer the idea of setting to music a popular story concerning mistaken identities.

This time, too, the same librettist who had been Mozart's successful partner in two previous collaborations was available. With Da Ponte, Mozart could be certain that the ticklish subject in question would be treated with wit and grace; the plot involved the attempts at seducing two maidens by the very men (in disguise) to whom they are betrothed. Unlike the earlier *Figaro* and *Don Giovanni*, in which Da Ponte based his librettos on existing sources, here the librettist had to rely on his own creative powers. In spite of the inherent improbabilities, he succeeded in producing an amusing, lively, theatrically effective plot.

• • •

Opera buffa in 2 acts. Libretto by Lorenzo da Ponte. *Première:* Hofburgtheater, Vienna, 1790.

Characters: Fiordiligi (soprano); Dorabella, her sister (mezzo-soprano); Guglielmo, Fiordiligi's suitor (baritone); Ferrando, Dorabella's suitor (tenor); Don Alfonso, bachelor (baritone); Despina, the sisters' maid (soprano).

Locale: Naples. *Time:* Eighteenth century.

• • •

Act I, scene 1. The young officers Ferrando and Guglielmo have joined their friend Alfonso on the terrace of a coffee house. As they sing the praises of their virtuous fiancées, Alfonso states that there is no such thing as fidelity in a woman. Every girl can be seduced if the right technique is applied. In order to prove this, he proposes a wager: within a twenty-four-hour period each of the men is to test the constancy of the other's betrothed. Convinced that they will win the bet, the officers accept the challenge cheerfully.

Scene 2. Alfonso brings the maidens the news that their suitors have been ordered to battle and must depart at once. The officers enter and all four give vent to declarations of love in a tearful farewell. Alfonso, an ironic smile on his lips, witnesses this touching scene. The maid Despina is less moved, and assures the girls that men do not deserve such treatment. Now Alfonso sets his plan in motion. He coaxes Despina into helping him introduce two young men to the girls; these strangers have supposedly fallen in love with the sisters. Ferrando and Guglielmo reappear, this time disguised as rich Albanians. The girls reject their attentions and order the would-be lovers to leave at once. Alfonso returns and greets the "Albanians" as if they were his closest friends, but the sisters do not yield. He and Despina then plot a more effective strategy.

Scene 3. The "Albanians" come upon the sisters in the garden and in extreme desperation declare their intention to commit suicide because of their unrequited love. The threat becomes seeming reality when each drinks the contents of a small bottle. Alfonso and Despina dash off to get a doctor to save the lovers, who have already fainted at the girls' feet. The sisters gaze upon the unconscious forms compassionately. Despina comes back disguised as a doctor and armed with a gigantic magnet that serves to revive the half-dead. The "Albanians" ask the girls for a kiss, but the request is refused.

Act II (in 4 scenes). Alfonso and Despina have hatched yet another plan of attack. Despina persuades Dorabella and Fiordiligi to keep a rendezvous with the "Albanians" that night in the garden, where they are greeted with a serenade. It is not long before Dorabella begins to weaken; she accepts the jewelry offered by her suitor and allows him to take Ferrando's locket in return. The disguised Ferrando continues to court Fiordiligi, but in vain. In order to avoid the increasing danger of an act of infidelity, Fiordiligi suggests to her sister that they follow their fiancés to battle. But when one of the "Albanians" assures her that if she goes he would surely kill himself, Fiordiligi too gives up her resistance. Ferrando and Guglielmo are disconsolate over the actions of their loved ones. With a cynical laugh, Alfonso explains, *"Così fan tutte"* ("So do all women"). The girls admit to Despina that they are prepared to wed the cavalier strangers that very night. Disguised as a notary, Despina intends to perform the wedding ceremony. Preparations are being made for a wedding feast when Alfonso brings the news that the officers have returned from battle unexpectedly. The "Albanians" and Despina exit hurriedly. The men re-enter in full uniform. Despina gets out of her predicament with the explanation that she has just returned from a masked ball. Alfonso reveals the marriage contract to the officers, whereupon they declare that they themselves are the "Albanians." Fiordiligi and Dorabella are ashamed of their own inconstancy, but Ferrando and Guglielmo forgive them. Alfonso has won his bet, and the two men expose him as the instigator of the dangerous plot.

don

Giovanni

DON GIOVANNI

After the rather cool reception first accorded *Le Nozze di Figaro* in Vienna, the work was so successful in Prague that the city's impresario Bondini immediately commissioned another opera from Wolfgang Amadeus Mozart (1756-1791). Encouraged by the artistic results of his partnership with Lorenzo da Ponte, the composer did not hesitate to turn to the same librettist again. There is little doubt that Da Ponte's theatrical instinct stimulated Mozart's musical fantasy to the highest degree. *Don Giovanni* was labeled by the composer, *dramma giocosa;* this indicates that Mozart wished the opera to be considered a comedy, despite the serious and even tragic elements in the plot. It is clear, therefore, that the epilogue, sometimes omitted in the past, should be restored and played before the curtain.

Mozart composed the overture, dramatically and musically the most important of his opera preludes, the night before the dress rehearsal. The manuscript score, written with hardly a correction, remains a testament to Mozart's genius. The overture begins with heavy, solemn woodwind chords that forecast the appearance of the stone guest at Don Giovanni's supper. The grim mood of the introduction is soon obliterated by a lively allegro melody in the violins, which reinforces the light character of the work. Many numbers in *Don Giovanni* have achieved popularity of a high order. One need mention only the "catalogue" aria, the minuet played by three separate orchestras in the ballroom, the duet of Don Giovanni and Zerlina, "*Là ci darem la mano*" ("Give me your hand"), Don Giovanni's "champagne" aria, and his serenade in front of Donna Elvira's house. The complex ensembles of the first-act finale, in which all the characters retain their individuality, and the grandiose spectral scene of Don Giovanni's downfall, have not been surpassed even by Mozart.

•   •   •

Opera in 2 acts. Libretto by Lorenzo da Ponte, based on Giovanni Bertati's play of the same name. *Première:* National Theater, Prague, 1787.

Characters: Don Giovanni, Castilian nobleman (baritone or bass); Leporello, his servant (bass); Don Pedro, Commandant of Seville (bass); Donna Anna, his daughter (soprano); Ottavio, her fiancé (tenor); Donna Elvira (soprano); Masetto, a peasant (bass); Zerlina, his promised bride (soprano).

Locale: In and near Seville. *Time:* Seventeenth century.

•   •   •

Act I, scene 1. Leporello stands watch in front of the palace of the Commandant while Don Giovanni attempts to seduce Donna Anna. When the latter cries for help, Don Giovanni flees. The Commandant pursues the intruder and is killed by him in a duel. Donna Anna's fiancé, Don Ottavio, rushes in and, seeing the dead body, swears to avenge the crime.

Scene 2. Unmoved by Leporello's warnings, Don Giovanni turns to new adventures. On the street he sees a veiled lady, Donna Elvira, who is searching for the man who betrayed her. She recognizes Don Giovanni as the faithless one. Promising that his servant will explain everything, Don Giovanni disappears. Leporello recounts the endless catalogue of Don Giovanni's love affairs. Elvira, enraged, wishes for revenge, though she still loves the scoundrel.

Scene 3. Don Giovanni and Leporello come upon the wedding festivities for Masetto and Zerlina. The incorrigible Don Giovanni wastes no time in attracting the attention of Masetto's pretty little fiancée. He invites the entire party to further celebrations at his castle. In order to be alone with Zerlina, Don Giovanni suggests that Masetto go ahead with the other peasants. Just as he is about to ensnare Zerlina, he is interrupted by Elvira. Donna Anna and Don Ottavio appear and ask Don Giovanni, whom they do not recognize, to aid them in their search for the Commandant's murderer. Once again Donna Elvira interrupts and warns the couple against Don Giovanni. After Donna Elvira and Don Giovanni leave, Donna Anna tells Ottavio that she has recognized Don Giovanni's voice, and that he is the murderer of her father.

Scene 4. Don Giovanni gives Leporello instructions for the feast. In the garden Zerlina tries to convince the jealous Masetto that her meeting with Don Giovanni was innocent. When Don Giovanni appears he resumes his game of love with Zerlina while Masetto, who has hidden himself, observes all. When the enraged Masetto confronts Don Giovanni, the latter offers the naïve Masetto the cool explanation that his actions merely reflect courtly politeness toward womanhood. Donna Anna, Donna Elvira, and Ottavio, all in masks, appear and are invited by Don Giovanni to take part in the festivities. Taking advantage of a moment when the guests are dancing a minuet, Don Giovanni entices Zerlina into an anteroom. Her cries for help are heard. Don Giovanni, retreating from the anteroom, summons enough audacity to accuse Leporello of having

forced his attention upon Zerlina. Donna Anna, Donna Elvira, and Don Ottavio, filled with revulsion, close in on Don Giovanni, who draws his sword and makes his escape.

Act II, scene 1. Don Giovanni appears at night in front of Donna Elvira's house. His object this time is Elvira's maid. In order to facilitate his conquest, he exchanges hat and cloak with Leporello. Elvira appears on the balcony and is persuaded by Don Giovanni's renewed declaration of love to keep a rendezvous in front of the house. Don Giovanni leads her to Leporello, in Don Giovanni's attire, thus clearing the way for his own serenade to the pretty maid. Masetto enters with some friends whom he has enlisted to help him avenge the attempted seduction of Zerlina. Don Giovanni, not recognized in Leporello's garments, declares his willingness to help them. After he has sent the others off, he falls upon the unsuspecting Masetto and gives him a beating. Zerlina responds to Masetto's cries and consoles him.

Scene 2. Donna Elvira and Leporello, the latter still disguised as Don Giovanni, come to the gates of Donna Anna's palace. Here they meet Anna and Ottavio, and are soon joined by Masetto and Zerlina. Leporello, realizing his danger, discards his disguise and declares that he has not the slightest desire to atone for his master's misdeeds. Now Ottavio realizes who the guilty one is and swears to bring about his punishment.

Scene 3. Don Giovanni finds himself in a cemetery at the foot of the Commandant's monument. He is joined by Leporello. In a fit of reckless insolence, Don Giovanni orders his servant to invite the stone statue to supper. The stone figure nods its head in acceptance.

Scene 4. In Donna Anna's house, Don Ottavio begs his beloved to marry him at last. She asks her suitor to wait a year so that she may have time to recover from the pain of her father's death.

Scene 5. Don Giovanni dines at a generously laden table while a band of musicians serenades him. Donna Elvira enters and begs Don Giovanni to repent a final time, but she is rebuffed cynically. At the door she screams, and Leporello, horror-stricken, exclaims that the statue of the Commandant is standing on the threshold. The guests leave. The statue cannot eat of earthly food, but invites Don Giovanni to come and eat with him. Don Giovanni gives the stone guest his hand, but at the statue's urging he refuses scornfully to repent his wrongdoings. The statue disappears, and Don Giovanni falls as the castle burns.

The stone statue of the murdered Commendatore comes to Giovanni's dinner: Ludwig Weber at the Vienna State Opera.

Falstaff

When well into his seventies, Giuseppe Verdi (1813-
1901) found that he was tiring easily, and deep in his
mind the belief was taking root that he had come to the
end of his career. His work progressed slowly, and yet,
true to his peasant background, he still felt relatively strong
and well. Boito suggested that together they give *The
Merry Wives of Windsor* a new musical vitality, and the
composer considered the project because he wanted to be
confronted with a real spiritual and musical challenge. He
informed Boito that for forty years he had been thinking
of writing a comic opera. Verdi began the work; he regu-
larly dedicated several hours a day to the new project.
The more he wrote, the more deeply he became involved
in it.

Nearing eighty, Verdi began the La Scala rehearsals for
Falstaff with extraordinary energy. He supervised every
detail of the preparations, just as he had as a young man.
As he put the finishing touches on the score, he was convinced that he was terminating his active participation in
the world of opera.

Falstaff reflects neither the composer's receding physical
strength, nor his frequent depression brought on by lone-
liness. Rather, it establishes an amazing new high point of
his creative powers. Verdi's fear that he might not capture
"the cheerful mood, the right mood, above all, the authen-
tic mood" was without basis. Verdi constructed this final
work of his operatic career with advanced means of musical architecture and characterization; his work is unique in
its finesse, simplicity, and impact.

•   •   •

Lyric comedy in 3 acts. Libretto by Arrigo Boito, based
on Shakespeare's *The Merry Wives of Windsor* and *King
Henry IV*. *Première:* La Scala, Milan, 1893.

Characters: Sir John Falstaff (baritone); Ford, wealthy
burgher (baritone); Alice Ford, his wife (soprano); Anne,
their daughter (soprano); Fenton, Anne's suitor (tenor);
Meg Page (mezzo-soprano); Dame Quickly (mezzo-soprano or contralto); Dr. Caius, physician (tenor); Bardolph, one of Falstaff's followers (tenor); Pistol, another
henchman (bass); innkeeper.

Locale: Windsor and environs, England. *Time:* Fifteenth
century.

•   •   •

Act I, scene 1.   Sir John Falstaff, Bardolph, and Pistol are drinking at the Garter Inn. Dr. Caius appears and, enraged, accuses Falstaff of having beaten his servants and stolen his horses. Furthermore, the doctor claims, Bardolph and Pistol robbed him. Falstaff dismisses Dr. Caius with a mocking "Amen."

Falstaff is given a bill by the host of the inn, but he is unable to pay it. So he devises a plot to get the money, telling Bardolph and Pistol how two jolly wives of Windsor —Alice Ford and Meg Page—have been attracted to him. He explains they control their husbands' purses, and he intends to oblige them to order to get money from them. Falstaff then says he has written both of them a letter and asks Bardolph and Pistol to deliver them. But the rascals refuse the assignment on "grounds of honor." Angered by their excuses, Falstaff chases the pair out the door with a broom.

Scene 2. Mrs. Ford is talking in her garden with Mrs. Page. They compare their respective love letters, and with much amusement realize that the two are identical. They are joined by Anne Ford and the gossipy Dame Quickly. The four decide to make Sir John the laughing stock of Windsor. Fenton and Ford also enter the plot. Dame Quickly agrees to bring Falstaff a letter inviting him to a rendezvous with Mrs. Ford. Informed by Bardolph and Pistol of Falstaff's love letter, Ford decides to go and meet the knight at the Garter Inn. He will disguise himself for the occasion. The intriguers separate amid laughter.

Act II, scene 1. Dame Quickly persuades Falstaff to come to Ford's house at a time when Ford is away. Ford himself appears next and, using a false name, begs Falstaff to help him win the affections of Mrs. Ford, who has thus far spurned him. A purse of money makes Falstaff eager to accept the offer. He admits to his new-found friend that he himself is interested in the lady in question. As Falstaff exits to change his clothes for the adventure, Ford, left alone, is suddenly overcome with anger.

Singing "Is it a dream? Or is it real?" he muses on the infidelity of women and then swears revenge on Falstaff and his own wife. But the scene ends on a note of comedy, with he and Falstaff bowing to each other and leaving together arm-in-arm.

Scene 2. Anne Ford gives vent to her fury brought on by her father's desire to force her into a marriage with the hated Dr. Caius. She agrees to join in the plot against Falstaff, provided the women help her fulfill her wish to marry Fenton. A gigantic laundry basket is brought in.

Falstaff appears and immediately tries to win Mrs. Ford's affections. At this moment, Dame Quickly and Mrs. Page enter to announce the unexpected return of Ford. Falstaff quickly hides behind a screen. Accompanied by Bardolph, Pistol, Caius, and Fenton, Ford begins a wild search for the intruder. The jealous husband even looks through the laundry basket. When the search is continued in another room, the ladies fetch Falstaff from his hiding-place and put him into the laundry basket. Ford bursts into the room again, and looks behind the screen. He surprises Fenton and Anne, who have taken advantage of the chaos to snatch a few tender kisses. Having filled the basket to the top with dirty laundry, the wives summon two servants and order them to empty it into the Thames. All run to the window, and watch when the fat knight, soaked to the skin, crawls to shore.

Act III, scene 1. Falstaff is seated at the Inn, meditating on the cruelty of the world. Dame Quickly appears with a new invitation from Mrs. Ford. This time, however, the rendezvous shall take place—for the sake of safety— at Windsor Park at midnight. Falstaff accepts cheerfully, and leaves with Dame Quickly to make further arrangements. Now the conspirators appear. They decide to stage a masquerade with nymphs and goblins. Ford tells Dr. Caius that he can recognize Anne by her white dress and green veil. Tonight he will approve their engagement.

Scene 2. All those involved in the plot appear in various fantastic costumes, and hide. At the stroke of twelve, Falstaff makes his entrance, wearing a wide cloak and a headgear on which antlers are fastened. He is attacked from all sides by taunts and blows. When the commotion has died down, Ford gives a disguised couple (as he thinks, his daughter Anne and Dr. Caius) to each other in betrothal; after which another couple (actually Anne and Fenton) ask for the same ceremony. In the first couple, Bardolph had been disguised as Anne. When the disguises have been put aside, Ford accepts his defeat, and the general frolicsome spirit becomes contagious. Falstaff soon joins the merry moral: *"Tutto nel mondo è burla"* ("All the world is but a joke").

Everyone is reconciled in the magic of the night in the grand finale, and Verdi ends his career with a beautiful fugue in nine parts.

Alice Ford (Irmgard Armgard) and Meg Page (Diana Eustrati) compare love letters from Falstaff. Quickly (Gertrud Stilo) and Nanetta look on. Komische Oper, East Berlin.

FAUST

FAUST

Charles Gounod (1818-1893) suffered the same fate as a number of other famous opera composers. Only one of his stage works, *Faust,* has withstood the test of time. In the course of a modest professional life as church organist and composer of sacred music, Gounod met the celebrated opera singer, Pauline Viardot. She suggested that he venture into the field of opera and promised to sing the leading role. Gounod wrote *Sappho,* and the singer kept her word. But in spite of this great artist's participation, the work was not very successful. Not discouraged by two more failures, Gounod set to work on a libretto based on Goethe's *Faust,* supplied to him by Jules Barbier and Michel Carré. Even though the libretto closely follows Goethe's drama, its plot and language were to some extent adapted to the taste of the French opera public of the time. When first performed at the Theatre Lyrique in Paris in 1859, the work was received with enthusiasm. Since then its attractive melodies and its moving plot have assured it a permanent place in the repertoire of many opera houses. Among the musical highlights of *Faust* are Marguerite's richly embellished "Jewel Song," the gripping *Dies irae* in the church, the moving scene between Faust and Marguerite in the prison cell, and the angels' chorus accompanying Marguerite's death.

Gounod never again reached this summit in his career as a composer of opera. Eight years after *Faust* he had a *succès d'estime* with *Roméo et Juliette,* which still enjoys a certain popularity, especially in France. Having had no more luck with additional operas, Gounod again turned to the composition of instrumental and church music. The year of his death, 1893, saw the creation of a *Requiem* that ranks among the best of his works.

* * *

Opera in 5 acts. Libretto by Jules Barbier and Michel Carré, after Goethe's drama. *Première:* Paris, 1859.

Characters: Faust (tenor); Méphistophélès (bass); Marguerite (soprano); Valentin, her brother (baritone); Martha Schwertlein, her neighbor (mezzo-soprano); Siebel, youth (mezzo-soprano); Wagner, student (baritone).

Locale: Germany. *Time:* Sixteenth century.

* * *

Marguerite (Victoria de los Angeles) and Faust (Jan Peerce) sing the great love duet in a Metropolitan Opera Production.

Act I. The old scientist, Faust, sits in his study. He thinks of his senselessly wasted life and decides to end it by committing suicide. When he lifts a glass with the poisoned drink to his lips he hears the merry singing of young girls and country folk going to work. Angry with himself and seized by remorse, Faust in desperation invokes the devil. The devil appears in the guise of a young nobleman. Méphistophélès promises to fulfill all of Faust's wishes, especially his desire to be young again, on condition that, later on, he forfeit his soul to him. When Faust hesitates, Méphistophélès conjures up the vision of a beautiful girl (Marguerite). Dazzled by the apparition, Faust agrees to the pact. A magic potion at once transforms him into a handsome young man. The tempter promises the happy Faust to arrange a meeting with the girl he has just seen.

Act II. The colorful activity on the town's fairground where students are singing a merry song is suddenly interrupted by Méphistophélès' appearance. He sings a cynical

Méphistophélès (Norman Scott) cruelly provokes Valentin (Walter Cassel, center) to challenge him to a duel, as Siebel

hymn to the power of gold. Then, reading Valentin's palm, he prophesies his early death, and also tells Siebel that the flowers for Marguerite will immediately wilt in his hand. From a glass of wine the devil causes the figure of Bacchus to rise, and in sneering words he drinks a toast to Valentin's sister, Marguerite. Outraged, Valentin threatens Méphistophélès with his sword, but his weapon breaks in two pieces. Soldiers who are standing nearby cross their swords, forcing the evil one to retreat. As people begin to dance, Faust appears. He offers to accompany Marguerite to church. She declines, but Méphistophélès assures Faust that his desire will yet find fulfillment.

Act III. Siebel is picking flowers in Marguerite's garden, but they wilt at once. He breaks the spell by dipping his fingers in holy water, and he places his bouquet before the door of Marguerite's house. In order to displace the unwelcome admirer, Méphistophélès conjures up a treasure of jewels. Marguerite enters the garden occupied with thoughts of the young man she had met earlier. She begins

(Francis Bible, right) draws his sword while the villagers look on. New York City Opera production at the City Center.

to spin and sings the song, "*Il était un Roi de Thulé*" ("Once a King in Thule"). Suddenly she discovers the jewel box and delightedly puts on some of the jewelry. To give Faust the opportunity to approach Marguerite without being disturbed, Méphistophélès talks with her neighbor, Martha, and declares his newly awakened love for her, though he voices insulting asides about her. Marguerite, who has already fallen in love with Faust, asks Méphistophélès to leave her. He invokes the magic spell of the night to bewitch her senses. When Marguerite opens her window and confides her love to the stars, Faust rushes into her arms while Méphistophélès retreats with devilish laughter.

Act IV, scene 1. Marguerite is tortured by fear and remorse for having given herself to Faust. Seeking comfort and forgiveness in prayer, she takes refuge in the church. There, too, the devil pursues her and taunts her so that her conscience cannot rest. With an outcry she breaks down.

Scene 2. The soldiers return from battle singing triumphantly. Among them is Valentin. When he asks about his sister Marguerite, he gets only evasive answers from Siebel. His suspicion aroused by a sarcastic serenade sung by Méphistophélès, who arrives with Faust, Valentin challenges Faust to a duel and is fatally wounded. Dying, he blames his sister, who bends over him, for all the misfortune.

Act V, scene 1. To make Faust forget the injury he has done to Marguerite, Méphistophélès takes him to a lonely spot on the summit of the Brocken, in the Harz Mountains where he parades beautiful women in Walpurgis Night festivities. When Marguerite appears to Faust in a vision with a red line around her neck as though caused by the executioner's ax, Faust entreats the devil to take him back to his beloved.

Scene 2. Marguerite in despair has murdered her newborn child and awaits her execution in prison. Faust and Méphistophélès gain entrance to the dungeon. Marguerite is overjoyed at the reunion with her beloved. But she does not agree to Méphistophélès' plan to escape, because she wants to take the punishment upon herself. Imploring Heaven to redeem her, she dies. In scornful triumph Méphistophélès cries: "She is judged." But a heavenly choir sings: "She is saved."

Noted Méphistophélès of the Metropolitan Opera: Ezio Pinza.

There is hardly a great master whose creative process was accompanied by such long inner struggle for perfection as was that of Ludwig van Beethoven (1770-1827). His sketches and extensive corrections, even in finished manuscripts, show how difficult it was for him to cast his musical ideas into a satisfactory form. His only opera, *Fidelio*, bears witness to his profound struggle.

The original title of the work was *Leonore*. The libretto follows closely the French original, *Léonore, ou l'amour conjugal*. With a lack of concern typical of the period, the librettist Sonnleithner appropriated the subject matter, and, much to Beethoven's chagrin, changed the title to *Fidelio* so as to avoid confusion with still another opera, *Leonora*, by Ferdinard Paer. Before an audience consisting largely of officers of Napoleon's army, Beethoven's work found a lukewarm reception. In numerous discussions with his friends, Beethoven was persuaded to make far-reaching changes and to contract the three acts into two. Still dissatisfied with the result, he turned to the librettist Treitschke, who then prepared the final version. The long deliberation concerning the structure of the opera brought forth no less than four overtures. The third, greatest and

The prisoners, afraid of the guards, yet happy to breathe fresh air, march in slowly and sing the highly emotional Prisoners'

by far the most significant, is played in many opera houses during the change of scene in the second act. It is also one of the most grandiose and most frequently performed concert overtures.

Beethoven's longing for marriage never was fulfilled. It found its touching artistic expression in this work, which represents a magnificent hymn in praise of indestructible love between husband and wife. There is hardly a dramatic soprano who would not count the aria referring to Pizarro, and the duet with Florestan, among the finest and most effective parts of her repertoire.

•   •   •

Opera in 2 acts. Libretto by Joseph Sonnleithner and Georg Friedrich Treitschke, after the drama by Jean Nicolas Bouilly. *Première:* Vienna, 1805. *First performance of the second version:* Vienna, 1806. *First performance of the third version:* Vienna, 1814.

Characters: Florestan (tenor); Léonore, his wife, disguised as Fidelio (soprano); Don Fernando, Minister of State (bass); Don Pizarro, governor of the state prison (baritone); Rocco, jailer (bass); Marzelline, his daughter

Chorus, in Harry Buckwitz's production at the Municipal Opera of Frankfurt. The set and costumes are by Franz Mertz.

(soprano); Jacquino, his helper (tenor); prisoners (tenor and bass); prisoners, guards, people.

Locale: State prison near Seville. *Time:* Eighteenth century.

•   •   •

Act I.   Jacquino is in love with Marzelline and tries to persuade her to marry him. But she feels a deep affection for Fidelio, her father's new helper. However, the helper actually is Léonore, who, disguised as a young man, wants to accomplish the liberation of her husband who has been unjustly imprisoned by the governor of the state prison. Rocco, the jailer, fully approves of his daughter's choice, and permits Fidelio to accompany him on his rounds of the cells. But he cannot take him to the dungeon of one particular prisoner (Florestan), who has aroused the hatred of the governor, Pizarro. The governor appears and learns from a letter that the Minister, Don Fernando, will inspect the prison. He therefore decides to dispose once and for all of Florestan, who knows of his many crimes and might reveal them. Since Rocco refuses to commit murder, Pizarro himself will deal the fatal blow. Fidelio overhears the conversation. Hoping for a chance to communicate with her husband, she persuades Rocco to permit the prisoners to get fresh air in the prison yard. The prisoners emerge from their dark cells and happily welcome the few minutes of sunshine granted to them. But Florestan is not among them.

Act II, scene 1.   In chains, Florestan languishes in the dungeon. Only the thought of his beloved wife keeps up his spirit. Rocco appears with Fidelio and begins to dig a grave in the cistern of the cellar. In the darkness of the deep vault the prisoner does not recognize the "young man" who offers him food and drink. Suddenly Pizarro turns up to commit the murder. When he draws the dagger for the mortal blow, Léonore stops him with the words, *"Toet' erst sein Weib!"* ("First kill his wife!"). At this moment the trumpet call outside announces the arrival of the Minister. Pizarro is forced to abandon his fiendish plan. Overcome with joy, husband and wife embrace.

Scene 2.   In the yard of the prison, the people gather to greet the Minister. In his address, Don Fernando promises to set free those unjustly imprisoned. Led by Rocco, Léonore and Florestan appear. Deeply moved, the Minister recognizes in Florestan a friend long believed dead. His chains are removed and Pizarro is arrested. All rejoice in a concluding chorus.

Lohengrin

82

LOHENGRIN

It is a tribute to the courage and especially to the high artistic insight of Franz Liszt, friend of Richard Wagner (1813-1883), that he dared to produce the opera *Lohengrin,* written by the outlawed composer. In 1849, Wagner had been an active participant in the revolution for greater political freedom that had broken out in Dresden and other cities. The production of *Lohengrin,* prepared to be given at the Dresden Opera House, had to be canceled when the house was destroyed by fire that resulted from the street fighting. When the revolutionary movement was put down by the troops, Wagner fled, and the Saxon government issued a warrant for the arrest of the court Kapellmeister. With a friend's passport and financial help from Liszt, Wagner arrived in Switzerland by a roundabout route. The opera was produced in Weimar in 1850. Ten years later Wagner was finally allowed to return to Germany, and in 1861 he heard his work in Vienna for the first time.

As with previous and later works, Wagner thoroughly investigated source material for *Lohengrin.* From the various renditions of the old Lohengrin legend, he wrote a poem of remarkable continuity. While in the *Flying Dutchman* and *Tannhäuser* the hero of the drama seeks redemption from the sins and afflictions of earthly life and desires to reach a higher, purer sphere, Lohengrin, coming from a superterrestrial region, aspires to love and understanding through a creature of this world. He believes that the final, inner union can be reached only if his name and origin remain hidden. Elsa is not endowed with the spiritual strength necessary for love without fathoming the character and origin of her beloved husband. Therefore Lohengrin's dream remains unfulfilled.

In the musical construction Wagner went far beyond the limitations that still held him back in *Tannhäuser.* Many of the stylistic characteristics of traditional opera are abandoned. In *Lohengrin* he takes another step away from the confines of strict melodic forms. In this way the work is indeed a forerunner of *Tristan* and *Parsifal.* The libretto and music possess an atmospheric power far greater than Wagner's earlier dramatic creations. The music drama is built on its own peculiar formal principles. It relies on no previously determined rules.

●   ●   ●

Opera in 2 acts. Première: Court Theater, Weimar, 1850. *Characters:* Henry the Fowler, King of Germany (bass);

Lohengrin, knight of the Grail (tenor); Elsa of Brabant (soprano); Friedrich of Telramund, Count of Brabant (baritone); Ortrud, his wife (mezzo-soprano or soprano); herald of the King (bass); Duke Gottfried, Elsa's brother (mute); 4 nobles of Brabant (tenor and bass); 4 pages (soprano and alto).

Locale: Antwerp and environs. *Time:* First half of the tenth century.

• • •

Act I. King Henry has arrived at Brabant on the banks of the Scheldt, near Antwerp, with his Saxon-Thuringian army to summon the nobles of the country to war against the rulers of eastern Europe. He wants first, however, to smooth over internal feuds in the country. The deceased Duke of Brabant had named Telramund as guardian of his two children, Elsa and Gottfried. Telramund accuses Elsa of murdering her brother. She had gone out with him and returned alone. For this reason he renounced marriage to Elsa, which he had promised to her father, and married Ortrud.

Elsa is summoned to defend herself. She explains in a trance that a knight who is willing to be her defender appeared to her in a dream. Twice the herald's summons resounds, while the knights and ladies pray. Suddenly a knight in shining armor approaches in a skiff drawn by a swan and declares that he is willing to assert Elsa's innocence. He attaches the condition that Elsa never ask his name or his origin. She vows to fulfill his request. The king commands a duel between Elsa's accuser and defender. Lohengrin defeats Telramund, but grants him his life.

Act II. Elsa and Lohengrin are to be married. Festive sounds come from the brightly lighted castle at Antwerp. Telramund and Ortrud stand in the dark courtyard. He accuses her of misleading him to play the part of plaintiff, causing him thereby to be robbed of his honor. He is sorry that he did not marry Elsa instead of her. Ortrud regards Telramund and herself as in no way defeated; she advises him to accuse Lohengrin of sorcery. She herself will entice Elsa to ask Lohengrin the forbidden question.

When Elsa appears on the balcony of her chamber, Telramund withdraws to leave the field to Ortrud. Ortrud unburdens her grief to Elsa with hypocritical words. Elsa comes down to the doorway to console her. Ortrud does her best to get Elsa to doubt her good fortune.

Day breaks. The servants appear, followed by the nobles who are to participate in the wedding festivities. Telramund hears from the herald that he has been banished and excommunicated, and that Lohengrin, as the protector of Brabant, is to lead the armies. Telramund confides to four of his retainers that he will accuse Lohengrin of imposture.

Elsa appears, accompanied by a large retinue, and prepares to enter the church. At the threshold, Ortrud suddenly confronts her and forbids her to take precedence. The agitated scene is interrupted by the appearance of the king and the wedding procession. Now Telramund takes up the fight and demands that Lohengrin state his "name, home, position, and title." Lohengrin is not willing to answer, even to the king. Elsa reassures him of her love, untarnished by any doubt. Escorted by the king and Lohengrin, she enters the church.

Act III, scene 1. King Henry and the guests lead the married couple into the bridal chamber. Left alone, Elsa and Lohengrin assure each other of their love. Although Lohengrin knows the name of his young wife, she does not know what to call him. He tries to calm her. Finally it is impossible for her to master her anxiety over the uncertainty and the seeming lack of trust on his part. In a vision, she suddenly sees the swan with the skiff, which is to take her beloved away again, and she asks the forbidden question. At this moment Telramund with four of his devoted knights rush into the chamber with drawn swords. Lohengrin kills Telramund with his sword. The terrified knights fall at Lohengrin's feet. With the cry, "Now all good fortune is over," he orders the slain man carried to the king's tribunal.

Scene 2. In deep sorrow, he declares himself ready to reply before the king to the question Elsa has put to him. The knights and their squires gather on the banks of the Scheldt. Lohengrin appears and recounts the slaying of Telramund. He says that Elsa has been persuaded to break her promise, and that he is Lohengrin, a Knight of the Holy Grail from the castle of Montsalvat and the son of Parsifal. He must now return home. He bids an emotional farewell to Elsa, who is beside herself. In wild triumph, Ortrud confronts Elsa and announces that she transformed Gottfried, the heir of Brabant, into a swan by a magic spell. As Lohengrin climbs into the skiff, a white dove descends upon it. Lohengrin loosens the swan's chain, and instantly Gottfried jumps onto the bank and is designated by Lohengrin as the ruler of Brabant. The dove has seized the chain and draws Lohengrin away in the skiff. Elsa, with the cry, "My husband," sinks lifeless into the arms of her brother.

Leonie Rysanek as Elsa von Brabant. Bayreuth Festival of 1958.

Lammermoor

With the light touch characteristic of many Italian composers of his period, Gaetano Donizetti (1797-1848) created within some thirty-five years no fewer than seventy operas. In addition, he wrote symphonies, string quartets, and church music. He even contracted to supply twelve operas within three years to the famous impresario, Domenico Barbaja, who for a number of years managed at the same time the Teatro San Carlo in Naples, La Scala in Milan, and the Kaerntnertor Theatre in Vienna. It is obvious that with such mass production the artistic results were uneven. Of his most popular operas, *L'Elisir d'Amore, Don Pasquale,* and the tragic opera *Lucia di Lammermoor* have maintained their place in opera repertoire. At the height of his career, shortly after the first performance of the opera *Catarina Cornaro* in Naples in 1844, Donizetti fell victim to a mental disturbance, and was committed to an institution in Ivry, near Paris. Four years later, in his native town of Bergamo, the disease finally resulted in his death.

Donizetti was a master of the style of *opera seria* as well as of *opera buffa,* and was equaled by few of his contemporaries. His melody falls agreeably on the ear, without becoming banal. The sentimental plot of *Lucia,* far re-

Lily Pons as Lucia in an early Metropolitan Opera production is shocked by the sudden appearance of her lover, whom she

moved from the spirit of our time, was placed by the composer in a musical environment that scarcely affords a psychologically convincing picture of the accumulation of tragic events. On the other hand, the score offers to the soloists, especially to the two central figures, Lucia and Edgar, a rich opportunity to display beautiful vocalism and technical virtuosity. For coloratura sopranos with dramatic ability, Lucia's "mad scene" in particular offers a chance to enrapture the public. The sextet in the second act, when the wedding ceremony is interrupted by Edgar's intrusion, is one of the composer's finest inspirations.

•   •   •

Opera in 3 acts. Libretto by Salvatore Cammarano, based on Sir Walter Scott's novel, "The Bride of Lammermoor." *Première:* Teatro San Carlo, Naples, 1835.

Characters: Lord Henry Ashton (baritone); Lucia, his sister (soprano); Sir Edgar Ravenswood (tenor); Lord Arthur Bucklaw (tenor); Raymond Bidebent, Lucia's tutor (bass); Alisa, Lucia's confidante (soprano); Norman, captain of the guard at Ravenswood (tenor).

Locale: Ravenswood Castle and the Tower of Wolfscrag in Scotland. *Time:* Late sixteenth century.

•   •   •

believed dead. The guests, assembled for the wedding, then express their conflicting emotions about the horrifying event.

Act I, scene 1.   A new reign in Scotland threatens land held by Lord Henry Ashton. He hopes to avert the danger by a marriage between his sister, Lucia, and the influential Lord Arthur Bucklaw. The guards, under the command of their captain, Norman, discover a stranger in the park of Ravenswood Castle. They suspect him to be Sir Edgar Ravenswood, whom Lord Ashton had cheated of his inheritance. Norman finds out that Lucia meets Edgar nightly, while pretending to visit her mother's grave. Lord Ashton swears to avenge the insult to the family honor.

Scene 2.   With Alisa, Lucia is waiting for Edgar in the park. She tells her confidante of a bad dream, in which her love came to an unhappy end. Edgar arrives at the appointed hour and informs Lucia that he has to travel to France immediately on an important political mission. Saying farewell, the lovers vow to be faithful to each other for life.

Act II.   Many months have passed since Edgar's departure. Henry Ashton prepares to carry out his plan of a marriage between Lucia and Bucklaw. He has intercepted all letters from Edgar, and he gives Lucia a forged letter that tells of her lover's faithlessness. In desperation, she consents to marry Bucklaw. At the moment when the marriage contract is being signed in the great hall of the castle, Edgar appears, at first unrecognized. Deeply hurt, he pushes Lucia away and insults her brother. As though in a trance, Lucia takes from her finger the ring Edgar gave her. He throws it to the floor and crushes it with his foot. Shielded only by Raymond from the attacking followers of Lord Ashton, he leaves the castle.

Act III, scene 1.   At Lammermoor Castle, the guests are present for the wedding festivities. Raymond enters and tells them he has found Arthur's dead body in the marriage chamber; he has been killed by Lucia with a sword. Lucia now enters, and the "mad scene" follows, in which she believes she hears Edgar's voice, and is once more united with him.

Scene 2.   In a ruined tower at Wolfscrag which commands a view of Lammermoor Castle, festively illuminated for the wedding, Edgar broods on his fate. When he hears from guests who have left the castle that Lucia is calling his name he decides to go to her, but Raymond appears and just then a bell begins to toll. Raymond tells him that it tolls for Lucia. For him, life without Lucia is worthless, and he stabs himself.

Joan Sutherland as Lucia in the Covent Garden production.

Madama

Giacomo Puccini (1858-1924) traveled to London in 1900 so that he could attend the English première of *Tosca*. There he saw the play, *Madame Butterfly*, by the New York theater director and dramatist, David Belasco. Although Puccini spoke no English, he understood enough of the action to realize that the play had tremendous musical potential. Immediately after the performance, he asked the author for permission to set it to music. Unlike many of his colleagues among Italian composers, Puccini did not work rapidly. Developing his sketches only sporadically, it took the composer more than three years to finish the *Butterfly* score.

The première at La Scala in Milan hardly reflected either the respect due a composer of Puccini's standing or the dignity of the house. The gallery in particular thwarted success with frequent offensive outbursts. While the audience made noisy protests against the melodies, which they considered old Puccini warmed over, Puccini sat in his box filled with bitterness. The composer Mascagni, a disgusted witness at this ugly occasion, declared, "The opera was a failure, but it will rise up again."

Although Puccini was enraged by the entire affair, he did recognize the need for a few revisions, and he made three acts of the opera's original two. In its altered form, *Madama Butterfly* is one of the most appealing and artistic portraits of a loving woman in the realm of modern opera.

•   •   •

Opera in 3 acts. Libretto by Giuseppe Giacosa and Luigi Illica, based on a play by David Belasco, who took the subject from a story by John Luther Long. *Première:* La Scala, Milan, 1904.

Characters: Cio-Cio-San, Madama Butterfly (soprano); Pinkerton, lieutenant in the U. S. Navy (tenor); Kate Pinkerton, his wife (mezzo-soprano); Sharpless, American Consul in Nagasaki (baritone); Goro, marriage broker (tenor); Prince Yamadori (baritone); The Bonze, Cio-Cio-San's uncle, a priest (bass); Suzuki, Cio-Cio-San's maid (mezzo-soprano); Trouble, Cio-Cio-San's son.

Locale: Nagasaki, Japan. *Time:* About 1900.

•   •   •

Act I. Guided by Goro, Pinkerton explores the country house where he intends to live with Cio-Cio-San. Goro introduces the servants, and informs Pinkerton that at least two dozen of the bride's relatives will attend the wedding. The American Consul, Sharpless, comes to pay his respects to his friend Pinkerton. Pinkerton is warned not to take his union with Butterfly too lightly. But the lieutenant seems intent only on making his stay in Japan as pleasant as possible. Sharpless is depressed by the blissful mood of the young Japanese girl as compared to Pinkerton's careless attitude. Butterfly states that her father is dead, and that she is fifteen years old. She shows Pinkerton her possessions, including some statuettes that are her "mascots." Suddenly becoming very serious, she also produces a case that holds the dagger with which her father committed suicide.

Butterfly's large family now appears, and the marriage contract is signed. Butterfly's uncle, The Bonze, bursts upon the scene. It is his intention to prevent the girl's marriage to a foreigner, which is contrary to his religious beliefs. Pinkerton dismisses the friends and relatives rudely. Night falls. Pinkerton is filled with desire, but the damning words of The Bonze ring in his bride's ears. The couple moves to the moonlit terrace, where they join in a duet filled with the longing of love.

Act II. Three years have passed. Pinkerton's ship has long since departed, and Butterfly, together with her small

The visitor, Sharpless (Warren Galjour) learns from Cio-Cio-San (Elaine Malbin) that Pinkerton has left behind a son (James Jordan) as well as a wife. NBC TV Opera production.

child, waits faithfully for her husband's return. She ignores the pessimism of her servant Suzuki. Accompanied by Goro, Sharpless comes with a letter. Goro has brought with him the Prince Yamadori, a desirable suitor who wants to marry Butterfly. Goro explains that the girl has the legal right to remarry, since Pinkerton has left her. Butterfly rejects this, for, in "her country, America" the marriage is binding.

When the disappointed Yamadori leaves, the Consul starts to disclose the contents of the letter: Pinkerton wants his freedom. Butterfly is dumbfounded; she summons her child and asks, "How could he forget this?" She reminds herself, however, that Pinkerton knows nothing of the child, who was born after his departure. Sharpless is so touched by Butterfly's tender devotion, that he cannot bring himself to tell her of Pinkerton's marriage to an American girl.

Goro, who had hidden himself in the garden, is still intent on getting Butterfly to marry Yamadori; he tells her that her child would find only derision in America. When she threatens him with the sacred dagger, Goro flees. Suddenly, a cannon is heard in the harbor. It is the sign that an American battleship is about to dock. Butterfly looks through a telescope, and identifies it as Pinkerton's ship. Almost overcome with joy, she decorates the room with flowers to welcome her beloved. In her bridal dress, she stands watch at an opening of the sliding screen door, while her servant and child doze off. A sad chorus from far away softly fills the room.

Act III. Dawn is breaking. Butterfly is still standing motionless in the same place. She carries her sleeping child to the next room. Sharpless and Pinkerton arrive. They enter, while Kate, Pinkerton's wife, walks nervously in the garden. Suzuki is told that Pinkerton and Kate wish to adopt the child and take him to America. When this becomes clear to Butterfly she is horrified. Suddenly she consents, under the conditions that Pinkerton call for his son in half an hour. Left alone, she takes a white veil from the cupboard, throws it over the screen, and draws the long, narrow dagger from its case. She reads the inscription: "Die with honor when it is impossible to live with honor." At this moment, the child rushes into the room. Butterfly drops the dagger, and kisses him passionately. She then sends the child outside to play. She grasps the knife once more and steps behind the screen. The knife is heard falling to the floor. Pinkerton's voice is heard. "Butterfly!" he cries. Cio-Cio-San drags herself as far as the door, where she falls dead.

Butterfly (Licia Albanese) bids farewell to her son, "Trouble."

The
Magic
Flute

For *Die Zauberflöte* (*The Magic Flute*), Wolfgang Amadeus Mozart (1756-1791) chose the theater director Schikaneder for his literary partner, and the libretto has frequently been criticized. Some have accused it of lacking unity and of containing long stretches of banality. The combination of farcical elements with solemn rituals has seemed a particularly troublesome contradiction.

The composer approached the opera with some hesitation, for he had never written a fantasy. Mozart is credited with the incorporation of the ethical ideas and goals of his Freemason fraternity, which serve to place the work on a higher humanitarian level than Schikaneder had intended.

Mozart managed to bridge admirably the juxtaposition of dissimilar elements in the libretto. The multi-faceted dramatic construction of *The Magic Flute* has made it an especially rewarding assignment for any producer. The overture, with its opening chords supported by tympani, and with the fugue that follows in the *allegro* section, established that Mozart had come a long way from the conventions of a popular fantasy.

•   •   •

Opera in 2 acts. Libretto by Johann Emanuel Schikaneder. *Première:* Theater auf der Wieden, Vienna, 1791.

Characters: Sarastro, high priest (bass); Tamino (tenor); priest, spokesman for Sarastro (bass); 2 priests (tenor and bass); Queen of the Night (soprano); Pamina, her daughter (soprano); 3 ladies of the Queen of the Night (2 sopranos, 1 mezzo-soprano); Papageno, a birdcatcher (baritone); Papagena (soprano); Monostatos, Moorish slave (tenor); 2 men in armor (tenor and bass); 3 genii; slaves, priests, Sarastro's retinue.

Locale: Memphis, Egypt. *Time:* In the days of Rameses I.

•   •   •

Act I, scene 1. Hunting, Tamino has lost his way and is chased by a gigantic snake. Three ladies of the Queen of the Night protect the exhausted prince and kill the monster with their spears. When Tamino revives, he sees Papageno before him. Papageno tells him of the Queen of the Night, and tries to convince Tamino that he, Papageno, strangled the snake. The three ladies reappear, put a lock on the lying lips of Papageno, and give Tamino a picture of the Queen of the Night's daughter. He immediately falls in love with the pretty maiden. Amid thunder and lightning, the Queen appears and exhorts Tamino to free her daughter Pamina from the demon who has taken her away. He gladly accepts the challenge. The ladies take the lock from Papageno's mouth, and the birdcatcher agrees to join Tamino. The Prince is given a magic flute, and Papageno is given equally effective silver bells. Led by three genii, the two start on their quest.

Scene 2. Monostatos has caught Pamina, escaped from her imprisonment. She faints from fear and excitement. Suddenly Papageno stands facing Monostatos; each is frightened of the other and they rush off in opposite directions. Pamina awakens and is told by the returning Papageno that a brave youth, Tamino, has been sent to liberate her.

Scene 3. The three genii then lead Tamino to the Temple of Isis; he attempts to enter. The spokesman blocks his path, and tells him that the high priest Sarastro is by no means the demon described by the Queen of the Night. Tamino begins to play his flute and is answered from a distance by Papageno's musical pipes. Papageno appears with Pamina; Monostatos and the other slaves prepare to attack. To hold them back, Papageno plays his silver bells, and the slaves are forced to dance to the magic tones. Amid the sounds of a festive march, Sarastro and his retinue come upon the scene. Regretfully, Pamina admits she had tried to escape. When Tamino is brought in by Monostatos, the girl and the youth fall into each other's arms. Monostatos demands a reward for his intervention, but instead, Sarastro orders a whipping for the Moor. The ideas of Freemasonry now come to the fore. Before Sarastro will grant approval to Tamino's union with Pamina, the youth must undergo certain trials to prove his strong character. Tamino and Papageno are led to the Temple of Trials.

Act II (in 10 scenes). Sarastro explains that Tamino and Pamina are destined for each other, and that the Queen of the Night had planned to destroy the temple. The assembled priests ask the deities of Isis and Osiris to bless the lovers.

Tamino declares his determination to meet even the strongest of challenges, but Papageno shows less enthusiasm. As their first test, the two are sworn to silence when they see Pamina. The three ladies try to induce Tamino to flee with them. He resists, and urges Papageno not to give in. The ladies are consigned to Hades by the priests.

Pamina, who has fallen asleep in the garden, is surprised by Monostatos. Just as he is about to kiss her, he is frightened away by the Queen of the Night, who appears amid thunder and lightning. The Queen gives her daughter

a dagger to kill Sarastro; she herself wants to rule over the priests and the Temple of the Sun. Though Sarastro knows of the malicious plot he grants forgiveness, for in the sacred portals of his temple vengeance is unknown.

Ignoring his oath of silence, Papageno chats with an old woman who has come his way. Suddenly, the old woman's shaky, cavernous voice changes, her tattered rags fall to the ground, and a young and appealing maiden—Papagena—stands before Papageno. She soon disappears, however, and the pleasure-seeking Papageno finds consolation in a basket of delicacies. Pamina appears, and is deeply troubled by the fact that Tamino will not speak to her.

Tamino and Pamina are led to Sarastro to say their last farewell to each other; this is yet another trial. Papageno also appears and, in his incorrigible search for pleasure, begs for a glass of good wine. Carefree, he begins to play on his magic bells. Thereupon the ugly old woman reappears, and again is transformed into the pretty Papagena. A priest separates the two immediately, and tells Papageno that this is his punishment for ignoring his oaths.

Pamina, desperate because of Tamino's apparent coolness and silence, decides to commit suicide. She is consoled, however, by the three genii, who promise that she will soon be united with Tamino.

Two men in armor now lead Tamino to a wild, rocky area where he is to undergo the final tests. He hears the voice of Pamina, who wishes to join her lover in his perilous wanderings. The magic flute accompanies the pair with its gentle tones, and Tamino and Pamina succeed in penetrating the Temple of Isis.

Papageno, overcome with grief at the loss of Papagena, has decided to hang himself on a tree. The three genii appear just in time, and advise him to play his magic bells. Papagena is attracted by the music, and, united, the two blissfully dream of their projected marriage and many children.

Filled with hatred for Sarastro, and led on by Monostatos, the Queen of the Night and her three ladies try to storm the temple. Her plan is thwarted by sudden thunder and lightning. Amid the brilliant light of the Temple of the Sun, Sarastro and his priests greet the happy couple, Tamino and Pamina. The opera ends with a hymn to beauty and wisdom.

The Genii reunite Papageno (Walter Berry) with his Papagena (Graziella Sciutti). Salzburg Festival Production of 1960.

The Marriage

of Figaro

THE MARRIAGE OF FIGARO

Wolfgang Amadeus Mozart (1756-1791) met Lorenzo da Ponte at a party given by the Baron Raimund Wetzlar von Plankenstern, who was the composer's long-time landlord and the "good and faithful friend" chosen to be the godfather of his first son, Raimund. This meeting, arranged by the host, led to a partnership that produced Mozart's three best opera librettos: *Le Nozze di Figaro, Don Giovanni,* and *Così Fan Tutte.*

At first Mozart remained reserved toward the young man of whose talents he had been previously informed. Only when Baron von Plankenstern guaranteed to finance the project in the event their work did not lead to a performance, did Mozart agree to the partnership. He accepted Da Ponte's suggestion of setting to music the play *Le Mariage de Figaro,* by Pierre Augustin Baron de Beaumarchais. The satirical comedy, a biting complaint against the ruling classes, had been forbidden by the Vienna censors. Only after Mozart played several excerpts for Emperor Joseph II, and only after all social and political attacks were removed, was permission granted for the Vienna première.

The libretto of *The Marriage of Figaro* stimulated Mozart's musico-dramatic genius to new heights. The featherlight overture, which begins with an infectious *presto,* provides an ideal introduction to the comic spirit of the work. Neither before *Figaro* nor after it, have figures of the rococo epoch been depicted with such finesse and impact. Nowhere in the realm of comic opera have wit, sensitivity, and warm-heartedness found such compelling expression. In the beauty of its melodies and in the architectural structures of the first- and fourth-act finales, *Figaro* has no parallels.

•　　　•　　　•

Opera in 4 acts. Libretto by Lorenzo da Ponte, based on the play by Pierre Beaumarchais. *Première:* Burgtheater, Vienna, 1786.

Characters: Count Almaviva (baritone); the Countess (soprano); Susanna, her maid, fiancée of Figaro (soprano); Figaro, the Count's valet (baritone or bass); Cherubino, page (soprano or mezzo-soprano); Marcellina, housekeeper at the castle of Count Almaviva (mezzo-soprano); Dr. Bartolo, physician (bass); Don Basilio, music master (tenor); Don Curzio, judge (tenor); Antonio, gardener (bass); Barbarina, his daughter (soprano).

Locale: The Count's castle near Seville. *Time:* Latter half of the eighteenth century.

•　　　•　　　•

Act I. Figaro takes the measurements for the room that is to be his bedroom upon his marriage to Susanna, while the latter tries on her bridal wreath. Susanna tells Figaro that the Count has given them a room near his own chambers so that he can be conveniently close to her. The Countess's bell calls Susanna from the room. Figaro leaves no doubt that he intends to undermine the plans of the Count. Upon Figaro's exit, Dr. Bartolo and Marcellina appear. Marcellina wants to force Figaro either to return the money he owes her or marry her.

Susanna reappears and bestows ironic compliments upon Marcellina, who, while being shown to the door, returns the courtesy with equal bite. Cherubino rushes in to air his plight to Susanna: the Count has discovered him at a rendezvous with Barbarina, and wants to dismiss him, but Cherubino is really infatuated with the young Countess. When the Count's voice is heard in the corridor, Cherubino hides behind a large chair. Almaviva promises Susanna a lovely wedding present on condition that she meet him in the palace park that night. When the Count hears the voice of the music master Basilio outside, he moves to hide behind the chair, and Susanna manages to allow Cherubino to slip from his hiding place and into the chair, where she covers him with a drape. Basilio asks the whereabouts of the Count and Cherubino, who were seen that morning in the vicinity. He drops some pointed allusions to the page's interest in the Countess. The Count, enraged, comes out of hiding and demands an explanation. The Count tells dramatically of how he caught Cherubino with Barbarina, snatches the drape from the chair and discovers Cherubino. But since Cherubino has overheard the Count's incriminating conversation with Susanna, Almaviva must be careful. He gives the page an officer's commission in the regiment commanded by him, and declares that the boy's departure is to take place that same day. Basilio reluctantly retracts the suspicions he expressed concerning Cherubino.

Figaro appears with a cheerful group of peasants. The Count is prepared to place on Susanna's head the veil symbolic of feminine virtue. Secretly, however, he hopes that Marcellina will appear in time to press her claims against Figaro. After the peasants have left, the Count departs. With good-natured mockery, Figaro offers Cherubino some advice on the glorious military career that awaits him.

Act II. In her chamber, the Countess expresses her grief over her husband's cooling love. Susanna enters with her fiancé. Figaro has conceived a plan: the Count is to receive an anonymous letter hinting at the infidelity of his wife, in order to make him jealous. Furthermore, Susanna is to give token acceptance to his invitation for the park rendezvous. In reality, however, the Count will meet Cherubino there dressed in the Countess's gown.

Cherubino is initiated into the plan and he tries on the Countess's clothing. In the process it is discovered that he has a ribbon belonging to the Countess. Suddenly there is a knock at the locked door. Cherubino disappears into the Countess's dressing room and Susanna leaves the room. The Count enters. When he hears a chair being overturned in the next room, he is suspicious and demands that the door be unlocked. The Countess refuses to give him the key on the grounds that Susanna is using the chamber to change her clothes; the Count leaves to get tools to force the door. He insists his wife accompany him, and bolts the door so no one can escape. Susanna comes out of hiding and releases Cherubino with her own key. The page makes an escape through the window and Susanna locks herself into the dressing room he has vacated.

The Count and Countess return. In desperation, the Countess admits that the page is in the room. Just as the Count draws his sword, the door opens and to the consternation of both Count and Countess, Susanna appears. The Count is contrite and willingly accepts the explanations for this strange situation. Just then the gardener Antonio comes to complain that an unknown person, probably Cherubino, has jumped out of the window and crushed the flower bed below. Figaro volunteers the information that he had found an important document, Cherubino's officer's commission. Since the Count had neglected to affix on it his official seal, he brought it back. Figaro claims further that the unexpected appearance of the Count so frightened him that he himself sprang from the window.

Marcellina, accompanied by Bartolo and Basilio, enters to remind Figaro that he has not made good his debt. She demands that he fulfill his promise to marry her. The Count refers the case to the judges. The Countess, Susanna, and Figaro anticipate the trial with concern; Marcellina, Bartolo, and Basilio look forward to their victory with exultation.

Act III. In a hall of the palace, Susanna tells the Count she will keep their rendezvous in the park. The judgment scene follows, and the judge, Don Curzio, reveals his decision: Figaro's choice is payment or marriage. In desperation Figaro defends himself with the claim that he

Lisa della Casa as the Countess Almaviva and Irmgard Seefried as her most lovable maid, Susanna. Salzburg Festival.

cannot marry without the permission of his parents, and he doesn't know who his parents are because he was abducted by robbers while still a baby. Marcellina and Bartolo recognize a birthmark on Figaro's arm and realize that he is their own long-lost illegitimate son. Marcellina persuades Bartolo to marry her, an act long overdue, and a double wedding is arranged.

Susanna returns with the Countess and together they compose Susanna's letter to the Count, in which the place of their secret meeting is proposed. A group of girls enters to give flowers to Almaviva and his wife; among them, the Count and Antonio discover Cherubino dressed as a girl. During the wedding ceremony, Susanna kneels before the Count so that he can place the bridal wreath on her head. In doing so, she slips him the *billet-doux*. The Count invites everyone to attend the wedding celebration.

Act IV. In the darkened park, Barbarina searches for a lost pin she was to have brought to the Count as a sign from Susanna.

Now begins an extraordinarily confusing intrigue, in which each of the main characters takes part: Figaro, who enters with Marcellina, expresses suspicion that the Count

Cherubino (Teresa Berganza) sings his charming love ballad entitled *Voi che sapete* to the Countess (Claire Watson), a

already wants to start an affair with Susanna. Barbarina appears in order to meet her lover Cherubino. Figaro summons Bartolo and Basilio as witnesses for Susanna's expected infidelity. Since the Countess and Susanna have switched costumes, Cherubino mistakes the Countess for her maid and demands a kiss. The enraged Count intercedes. The slap intended for Cherubino lands on the cheek of Figaro, who has suddenly come out of hiding. Cherubino flees. The Count thinks he is alone with Susanna. Figaro, on the other hand, assumes that the Countess awaits him. When he hears Susanna's bad imitation of the Countess's voice, he recognizes his bride; Susanna thinks that Figaro's attention is really directed toward the Countess, however, and rewards him with another slap.

After they have made up, Figaro and Susanna embark on a mock love scene with which they dupe the jealous Count. Just as the latter is about to reprimand the "Countess" (Susanna in disguise), the real Countess enters. The Count recognizes her and, full of contrition, begs for forgiveness. Everyone breathes easily. Happily they adjourn to the castle to celebrate the marriage of Susanna and Figaro, as well as that of Marcellina and Bartolo.

love ballad he has written himself. He is accompanied by Susanna (Graziella Sciutti) with a guitar. Holland Festival, 1961.

Die Meistersinger

Von Nürnberg

In his autobiography, *Mein Leben*, Richard Wagner (1813-1883) explains how the idea for a comedy based on the activities of the Mastersingers had fascinated him while he was taking the cure at Marienbad: ". . . Without knowing very much about Sachs and his poetic contemporaries, I conceived the idea, during one of my walks, of a droll scene in which the cobbler, in the capacity of a popular artisan-poet, makes the Marker sing, and, by the application of his hammer to his last, gives him a lesson by way of punishment for his pedantic misdeeds. . . . My whole Mastersingers comedy suddenly sprang into such vivid life within me that, as it was a particularly merry theme, not likely to overexcite me, I felt justified in disobeying my doctor's orders and putting it on paper." The Marienbad physician realized the impossibility of restraining an artist, gripped by the transports of creative inspiration, and advised a prompt termination of the cure.

In spite of this initial excitement, sixteen years passed before Wagner again took up the project. In the intervening time, the composer lived both his personal and artistic life through happy as well as sad episodes: his flight from Germany; the disappointment over the Paris première of *Tannhäuser;* the close relationship with Mathilde Wesendonck, full of so many sorrows; the painful parting from his wife, Minna; and, among other things, the highly successful première of *Lohengrin* in Weimar and the completion of *Tristan,* which had so aroused his most intimate emotions. Now, as he put it, "the spirit of quiet, smiling resignation" ruled over him. The humor of *Die Meistersinger* grew out of this basic mood. He sketched the poem in Paris during 1861-62 and began the composition in complete solitude at Biebrich am Rhein. He started work with the Prelude, not, as with most of the other operas, leaving composition of the overture to the end. The full score was completed October, 1867, at Triebschen, his home in Switzerland. The première took place in Munich in 1868, under Hans von Bülow.

* * *

Opera in 3 acts. Première: Court and National Theater, Munich, 1868.

Characters: Hans Sachs, shoemaker (bass-baritone); Veit Pogner, goldsmith (bass); Kunz Vogelgesang, furrier (tenor); Konrad Nachtigall, plumber (bass); Sixtus Beckmesser, town clerk (bass); Fritz Kothner, baker (bass); Balthasar Zorn, pewterer (tenor); Ulrich Eisslinger, grocer (tenor);

Beckmesser (Gerhard Pechner) searches Sachs' study for the prize song. Metropolitan Opera Production of the early 1950's.

Augustin Moser, tailor (tenor); Hermann Ortel, soap-maker (bass); Hans Schwarz, stocking weaver (bass); Hans Folz, coppersmith (bass); Walther von Stolzing, young knight from Franconia (tenor); David, apprentice to Sachs (tenor); Eva, Pogner's daughter (soprano); Magdalene, Eva's nurse (mezzo-soprano); night watchman (bass).

Locale: Nürnberg. *Time:* Mid-sixteenth century.

• • •

Act I. The Prelude, the most contrapuntal and inventive of all of Wagner's orchestral introductions, initiates the action. Vespers draw to an end in St. Katherine's Church. Walther von Stolzing watches Eva Pogner, and would like to find out whether she is engaged. He discovers that at a singing contest to be held the following day the victor will have a chance to win Eva's hand. In order to compete, Walther decides to join the Mastersingers' guild. Magdalene gives David the task of initiating the knight into the rules of the guild.

The apprentices set the place for the Masters' meeting. Pogner and Beckmesser are the first to appear. The town clerk looks at the knight suspiciously, but Pogner recommends that the knight be admitted to the guild that very day. He must, however, submit to an examination. After some discussion, the Masters allow him to take a test. Asked what he will sing, he announces a love song. Beckmesser has the job of Marker, chalking on a slate the transgressions against the Mastersingers' rules. Beckmesser's angry chalk marks finally leave no more room on the slate, and he displays the innumerable errors. Sachs alone supports Walther's cause. The Masters finally reach a negative verdict, and Walther leaves in haughty anger. The Mastersingers and apprentices also leave. Hans Sachs remains alone, deep in thought, and approaches the door with a gesture of resignation.

Act II. The scene opens on a narrow street. On one corner is Pogner's house; opposite is Hans Sachs' smaller house, with his workshop. David meets Magdalene and tells her of the knight's failure. The apprentices congratulate David on the choice of his bride, Magdalene, and then leave the square. Magdalene informs Eva of Walther's fruitless efforts. Eva turns to Hans Sachs, who is working in front of his door. He discovers her true feelings from her words to him; he sees that he, an aging widower, has no chance for her love, and he decides to help the young people. In the meantime, Magdalene has discovered that Beckmesser intends to serenade Eva that night. The women decide that Magdalene, dressed in Eva's clothes, shall receive the homage, while Eva will meet Walther under the linden tree.

Walther approaches and proposes to Eva that they elope immediately. Sachs opens the door of his shop, and the light illuminates the street. Eva and Walther hide. Beckmesser creeps in and begins his serenade, but Sachs continually interrupts him with hammering. Finally Beckmesser, in a rage, has to give up his singing, after Sachs has mischievously indicated by hammer strokes all his transgressions against the Mastersingers' rules. Awakened by the noise, the neighbors appear in the windows in their nightclothes. They come down to the street, and a wild fight develops. David takes the opportunity to give Beckmesser a sound thrashing, for he believes the serenade was meant for Magdalene. At the height of the fracas, Walther and Eva try to escape. Sachs quickly pulls Walther, who wants to force his way through with his sword, into his house, while Pogner hustles Eva into hers. The brawlers have finally dispersed. The beaten Beckmesser goes off, limping. When the street is empty, the sleepy night watchman appears and, blowing his horn, announces eleven o'clock.

Act III, scene 1. The next day Hans Sachs sits by the window in his workroom, reading a large folio. He tells David to get dressed for St. John's Day. Sachs meditates on the madness of all human actions. His thoughts are interrupted by the appearance of Walther, who tells Sachs of his marvelous dream of the night before, in which he saw his beloved. Sachs urges him to make the revelation in his dream his prize song, but he wants to make certain that he will adhere to the rules of the guild. Improvising, Walther begins to set the vision to words and music. Sachs explains to him the poetical form demanded by the Mastersingers and writes down the song in the correct manner. Scarcely have they left the workshop to dress for the festival, when Beckmesser peers through the door. He snoops around the room, and suddenly he sees on the table the song Sachs has written down. When he hears Sachs coming, he quickly puts the sheet in his pocket, in the belief that Sachs himself is going to use the song for the contest. He accuses Sachs of meaning to marry the daughter of the rich Pogner himself, and triumphantly draws the page from his pocket as proof. To put Beckmesser completely at ease, Sachs gives him the sheet with the permission to use it as he sees fit. He promises never to claim authorship. However, he advises Beckmesser to memorize the song well, for it is very difficult. Overjoyed, Beckmesser hurries away with the song.

Eva, in festive dress, enters the workshop and complains about a shoe that is too tight. As Sachs puts the shoe on a stretcher, Walther appears in the doorway. He and Eva look at each other with love. Eva is deeply concerned about Sachs, and throws her arms around his neck. Gently he admonishes her: he knows only too well the tragic story of Tristan and Isolde. He does not want to suffer the fate of King Marke. Magdalene and David enter in gala dress. After Sachs has made the apprentice into a journeyman through a slap on the cheek, according to ancient custom, everyone joins in a quintet: Eva and Walther sing of their happiness in love; Sachs of his renunciation; Magdalene and David of their approaching marriage. Then Sachs bids everyone hurry to the festival.

Scene 2. The guilds arrive with their banners. The last to appear are the Mastersingers. Then everyone joins in singing the hymn, "Awake!" which swells into a joyful homage to Sachs.

The first singer called is Beckmesser, who is still trying hurriedly to memorize Sachs's song. His performance is so ridiculous that he is laughed at: he distorts the words, which he does not understand, into senseless rhymes and furnishes them with a flowery melody, which he had already tried to use for the serenade honoring Eva. In rage, he flings the sheet at Sachs's feet and accuses him of tricking him with a bad song. Sachs rejects the accusation and explains that it has been ruined by Beckmesser through ignorance. As witness, he summons the true author of the song. Walther steps forward and, with mounting fervor, sings the prize song: "The morning light shines with rosy glow." Eva places a wreath on his head, and Pogner wants to complete the award by having Walther enter the Mastersinger guild. Walther refuses, and Sachs rises and admonishes him not to scorn the German Masters. While Eva now presses Walther's wreath on Sachs, Sachs takes a gold chain from Pogner and puts it around Walther's neck. The opera ends with an enthusiastic chorus in honor of Sachs.

Wieland Wagner's design for the contest scene of his grandfather's only comic opera, Bayreuth Festival Production, 1957.

According to the ancient saying, the gods take unto themselves at an early age those they love. Among the great composers, this applies particularly to Purcell, Pergolesi, Mozart, Schubert, and Vincenzo Bellini (1801-1835). Besides a long list of instrumental music and sacred vocal works, Bellini composed no fewer than eleven operas during less than a decade. Of these, *La Sonnambula, I Puritani,* and especially *Norma* have retained the favor of the opera public to this day. Bellini's strength is in the beauty, grace, and simplicity of a melodic line that is more lyrical than dramatic. The arias in his best works are structurely in perfect proportion. In *Norma*—as in *Il Pirata* and *La Sonnambula*—he was fortunate to have the collaboration of one of the ablest Italian librettists of his time, Felice Romani, who also supplied librettos for Donizetti, Rossini, and the young Verdi. *Norma* was Bellini's favorite work. Even Wagner, whose dramatic feeling and esthetics certainly were far removed from Bellini's style, praised this work highly.

Bellini came from an old family of musicians. His grandfather and father were choirmasters at the cathedral in Catania, Sicily. He gained his first lasting success with *Il Pirata* in 1827 at La Scala in Milan. After the high mark reached with *Norma* in 1831, *Beatrice di Tenda* found only a lukewarm reception. Deeply disappointed, Bellini

Pollione (John Alexander) is brought before the distraught

left Italy in 1833 and went to Paris, where he was acclaimed after the première of *I Puritani* in the Theatre des Italiens. While working on two new operas at the country home of an English admirer, the composer was stricken, and died in 1835.

•   •   •

Opera in 4 acts. Libretto by Felice Romani, based on a drama by Alexandre Soumet. *Première:* La Scala, Milan, 1831.

Characters: Norma, high priestess of the Druids (soprano); Oroveso, Arch-Druid, her father (bass); Pollione, Roman proconsul (tenor); Clotilda, Norma's confidante (soprano); Flavio, captain, Pollione's friend (tenor); Adalgisa, young priestess (soprano or mezzo-soprano); 2 children of Norma and Pollione (mute).

Locale: Gaul. *Time:* During the Roman occupation, about 50 B.C.

•   •   •

Act I, scene 1. In the sacred grove of the Druids, priests and soldiers led by Oroveso implore the deity for help against their Roman oppressors. After they have left the place of the religious ceremony, Pollione and Flavio appear. Pollione confides to his friend that Norma has vio-

Norma (Joan Sutherland). A Vancouver Opera Production.

lated the strict laws of her sect by giving her love to him. Two children were born of their union. Now his love for Norma has cooled, and he feels a strong passion for the young priestess Adalgisa. In a dream, Norma has appeared to him announcing her revenge.

Scene 2. The Druids are ready for open revolt against the Romans, but Norma restrains them from violence. She points out that Rome is already doomed to be destroyed through her own misdeeds. Therefore it would be as well to keep peace until then. She grieves that the Druids hate Pollione, whom she loves. After the Druids have left the grove, Adalgisa prays at the altar for release from her ill-starred love for the proconsul. Pollione, who has followed her, urges her to flee to Rome with him. Newly enchanted, she consents.

Act II. Norma is advised by Clotilda that Pollione plans to leave for Rome. Adalgisa, who wants to confide in Norma, admits her undying love for Pollione, not realizing that Norma is in love with the same man. Norma is deeply angered by this treachery, and when Pollione appears she hurls violent reproaches at him. All three unite their voices in a passionate debate of accusation and defense until a signal calls Norma to service in the temple.

Act III. Norma decides to kill Pollione, and to atone for the deed by sacrificing herself and her children. But after a struggle with her conscience she feels unable to kill the innocent children. Adalgisa meanwhile has arrived at the decision to give up Pollione and to persuade him to return to Norma.

Act IV. In the forest the Druids and soldiers make plans to throw off the Roman yoke. Now that Norma knows that Pollione will give her up, she fans the hatred against the oppressors. Pollione has been taken prisoner by Gallic soldiers. When Oroveso is about to kill him with a dagger, Norma seizes the weapon. She wants to spare her former lover if he is willing to renounce Adalgisa, but he rejects the demand. Now there is no hope left to Norma. She reproaches herself as the truly guilty one who betrayed her country, and orders the lighting of her funeral pyre. She asks her father to take care of the children. Pollione is overwhelmed by her nobility of spirit and resolves to die with her. Covered by the priests with a black veil, Norma takes Pollione's hand and walks with him into the purifying flames, accompanied by the chant of the priests.

Norma (Joan Sutherland) begs her father Oroveso (Richard Cross) to care for her children. Vancouver Opera Production.

OTELLO

Although Cammerano, Piave, Somma, and Ghislanzoni tried hard to make a place for themselves in the artistic world of Giuseppe Verdi (1813-1901), only in Arrigo Boito did the composer find a literary co-worker worthy of his genius. This fortunate meeting came at a time when Verdi was no longer thinking of writing operas. Boito himself had won considerable esteem for his opera *Mefistofele,* the text of which is based on Goethe's *Faust.* Verdi had already encountered Boito in 1862, but the relationship was tense because of Boito's low opinion of Italian music and composers. It was Verdi's publisher, Giulio Ricordi, who brought the two together again. Within a few days, Boito delivered his sketch for *Otello.*

Several years passed, however, before Verdi returned to the plan. Without thinking, Boito had remarked that he regretted not having set to music himself the text offered Verdi; this offended Verdi again. Out of wounded pride, he intended to return the libretto to Boito. The main reason for the long delay, however, lay elsewhere. "Too much time has passed. I am too old . . . I don't want the public to be justified in saying to me, 'Enough,' " Verdi wrote in a letter. Even in the year 1886, he wrote a pessimistic letter to the famous singer Francesco Tamagno, who desired the role of Otello: "I have not finished the opera, and even if it were finished, I have by no means made up my mind to have it performed."

For a long time it was the figure of Iago, not Otello, that monopolized Verdi's attention. He depicted with minute attention to detail the devilish character that fascinated him so; Iago was "thin and tall, with narrow lips, small eyes set close to the nose like those of an ape . . . nonbelieving, mocking that good and evil are for him one and the same."

Eventually, Verdi agreed to the opera's première at La Scala. But his decision was qualified by a number of difficult conditions. No one was to attend the rehearsals; the composer was to have the right to cancel the performance even after the dress rehearsal; and the entire artistic personnel was to be under the composer's jurisdiction. With a man of Verdi's fame, the theater director had no choice but to fulfill each condition.

Verdi had written no music since *Aïda* (1871), except for the revised *Simone Boccanegra* (1881). In this long period of silence, the composer had undergone several crucial style changes. Unlike many contemporaries, he refused to adapt the musico-dramatic language of Wagner. But the spirit of the "new artform" left its traces on him too. His music took on new emotional expression, characterizations achieved new finesse and richness. Today, *Otello* is considered among the best of Verdi's works.

•   •   •

Opera in 4 acts. Libretto by Arrigo Boito, after Shakespeare's drama *Othello. Première:* La Scala, Milan, 1887.

Characters: Otello, Moorish general in the service of Venice (tenor); Desdemona, his wife (soprano); Iago, Otello's aide (baritone); Cassio, Otello's lieutenant (tenor); Emilia, Iago's wife (mezzo-soprano); Montano, Otello's predecessor as governor of Cyprus (bass); Roderigo, Venetian gentleman (tenor); Lodovico, ambassador of Venice (bass); herald (bass).

Locale: Cyprus. *Time:* Fifteenth century.

•   •   •

Act I. During the period of her greatest power, Venice has occupied the island of Cyprus. The city's armies have conquered the Turks, and the commanding general, Otello, returns to the island in triumph. Greeted by his wife Desdemona, Otello enters his castle. Iago is enraged because Otello overlooked him and promoted Cassio to a higher military position; he is bent upon doing everything in his power to destroy Otello. He advises Roderigo, who is in love with Desdemona, to wait until she is weary of the "black monster with the protruding lips." He succeeds in getting Cassio drunk during the victory celebration. As Iago planned, Cassio precipitates a quarrel with Roderigo. Montano tries to separate the duelers, and is wounded by Cassio. Otello appears, and demotes Cassio from his new post as punishment for his behavior. The crowd leaves, leaving Otello alone with Desdemona. With tender words, they reassure each other of their love.

Act II. At a meeting in the governor's palace, Iago advises Cassio to ask Desdemona to intercede for him with Otello. When Otello enters, Iago awakes in him the seeds of suspicion against Desdemona, pointing out to him Cassio and Desdemona in conversation. Otello's jealousy is stimulated when his wife pleads with him to reconsider Cassio's plight. Desdemona wipes her husband's feverish brow with a handkerchief given her by Otello himself. He flings it to the floor and Emilia picks it up, but Iago quickly intercepts it. When Otello later asks Iago for proof of his suspicions, Iago describes the handkerchief, which he claims was found in Cassio's room while Cassio was asleep and was blissfully uttering Desdemona's name. Otello, together with Iago, swears vengeance.

Act III. Iago promises to give Otello further proof of

Desdemona's infidelity. When his wife once again tries to speak in Cassio's behalf, Otello hurls insults at her and demands to see the handkerchief he had given her. Unsuspecting, she explains that she does not have it with her at the moment. Otello continues to berate his wife, who flees from his insults. Cassio and Iago enter and, overheard by Otello from a concealed spot, they discuss a certain woman with whom Cassio is in love. When Cassio shows Iago a handkerchief he found in his room, Otello is convinced of Desdemona's guilt. He decides to kill her, and Iago declares himself willing to murder Cassio.

The Venetian ambassador Lodovico appears with a document from the Doge that orders Otello's return to Venice; Cassio is to replace him in Cyprus. Desdemona is upset at the news, and Otello interprets this as sorrow at being separated from Cassio. Losing control of himself, he hurls her to the floor, to the horror of the assembled crowd. Overcome with excitement, Otello collapses. Iago gives cynical vent to his triumph: "My poison has taken its effect. There lies the lion!"

Act IV. Desdemona retires to her chamber to find peace. Full of foreboding, she asks Emilia to place her wedding sheets on the bed. She thinks of an old, sad song about a willow tree, and sings it mournfully. She bids Emilia farewell. Left alone, she prays to the Virgin Mary, and then lies down on the bed. Otello enters through a secret door and observes his wife's sleeping form for a long time. He kisses her. When she awakens, Otello accuses her again of breaking her marriage vows. Her protestations of innocence only increase his fury. She asks that Cassio be summoned to speak for her, and Otello answers that Cassio will never speak again. He is about to kill her, but she begs him to give her time to pray. Now beside himself, Otello strangles her with his hands. There is knocking at the door, and Emilia bursts into the room to announce that Cassio has killed Roderigo. She discovers Otello's horrible deed, and hears the dying Desdemona say that she has killed herself, but that she is innocent. Otello says that it was he who killed her, and Emilia calls for help. Lodovico, Cassio, and Iago enter, followed by Montano, and Otello learns that he has been the victim of an infamous scheme. Iago escapes, pursued by attendants. In utter despair, Otello stabs himself fatally in the breast. He falls on Desdemona's body, and kisses her once more.

James McCracken as Otello at the Metropolitan Opera, 1963.

PAGLIACCI

The world fame of Ruggiero Leoncavallo (1858-1919) is based on a single work, *Pagliacci*. After studying at the Conservatory in Naples Leoncavallo had to endure many years of drudgery as music teacher and as conductor in small theaters. He had hoped to be able to change his artistic fortunes with two operas composed during this difficult period, *Chatterton* and *I Medici*, both to librettos written by himself. After the house of Ricordi in Milan had held the score of *I Medici* for three years without making any use of it, the composer submitted the work to the publisher Sonzogno. The latter had just offered a prize for a one-act opera, and the prize was won by Pietro Mascagni with a work called *Cavalleria Rusticana*. This was soon performed with great success. Sonzogno wanted to combine it with another short opera to make up a full evening's program, and he commissioned Leoncavallo to create a companion work for Mascagni's opera. Again his own librettist, the composer supplied the two-act opera, *Pagliacci*. It gained enthusiastic acclaim at the very first performance in Milan in 1892.

*   *   *

Opera in a prologue and 2 acts. Libretto by the composer. *Première:* Teatro dal Verme, Milan, 1892.

Characters: Canio, first clown (tenor); Nedda, Canio's wife (soprano); Tonio, second clown (baritone); Beppe, actor (tenor); Silvio, villager (baritone). During the play within the play the comedians take the roles of Pagliaccio, Columbina, Taddeo, and Arlecchino, respectively.

Locale: Near Montalto, Calabria. *Time:* The late 1860's.

*   *   *

Prologue: During the orchestral Prelude, Tonio, the hunchbacked clown, appears in front of the curtain and explains that the author of the play is presenting a story true to life. The outcome, he says, will manifest strong human emotions. "Let us go," Tonio cries. "The play begins."

Act I. A theatrical troupe directed by Canio arrives in the village square accompanied by great fanfare, and is welcomed joyfully by the populace. As Canio, Nedda, and Beppe, dressed in their pantomime costumes, enter on a donkey cart, the villagers sing a chorus of welcome. The

Eugene Tobin as Canio threatens Barbara Wittelsberger as Nedda in the production of the Municipal Opera, Frankfurt.

clown Tonio is about to assist Nedda with her baggage. Canio, her jealous husband, pushes him aside brusquely, and the villagers laugh and tease Tonio until he is about to leave. As he leaves, one of the company remarks that Tonio would like to be alone with Nedda. Canio, outraged, declares that, although as a clown on the stage he may play a deceived husband, it is different in real life. He says if he were to find his wife with a rival, he would avenge with blood. Villagers and actors disperse and Nedda remains alone, greatly frightened by her husband's threat. She wonders if her husband does suspect anything, as she is actually deceiving him with a young villager, Silvio. Tonio approaches and implores her favor, but is scornfully repulsed. When he persists, she strikes him with a whip. Vowing to avenge the disgrace, he rushes off. Meanwhile Silvio has come leaping over the wall and asks Nedda to leave her wretched life and go away with him. Tonio sees them together and quickly calls Nedda's husband from the inn. They return just as Silvio is fleeing, and Canio demands that Nedda name her lover. When she refuses, Canio draws his knife, but Beppe seizes it. Tonio slyly advises Canio to wait for the performance, for surely the lover will show up then. In a wild outburst of grief, Canio bewails the dual role he is forced to play as a man and as a comedian.

Act II. After the sunset, performance starts. Columbina (Nedda) awaits her lover, Arlecchino (Beppe). Taddeo (Tonio) enters the room and confesses his love to Columbina. He disappears when he hears Arlecchino's footsteps. After a merry meal, Arlecchino makes a quick exit through the window when Taddeo announces the arrival of Pagliaccio (Canio). Changing from stage play to real life, Canio furiously tells his wife he must know the name of her lover or she will die. Nedda, who wants to continue the comedy, assures him he is mistaken. The unsuspecting audience, somewhat confused but fascinated by the realism of the acting, applauds enthusiastically. Beppe tries to rush to the couple, but Tonio restrains him. Canio seizes a knife from the table and stabs Nedda in the back as she tries to escape into the audience. Silvio rushes forward, and as Nedda manages to speak the name, "Silvio," Canio draws his dagger and stabs Silvio. He then drops his knife, turns to the horrified crowd and manages to cry out, "The comedy is ended."

James McCracken as Canio in the Metropolitan Opera production, invites the Villagers to the evening's entertainment.

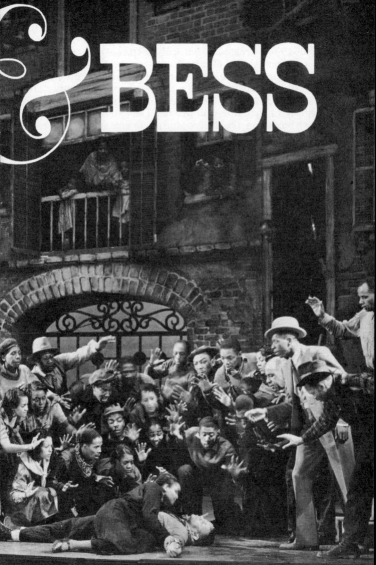

PORGY AND BESS

The contributions of the United States to the international opera world are limited to a few works of recent date. Among them, *Porgy and Bess* has enjoyed far-reaching success. With a sensitivity for folklore unequaled in the work of any comparable composer, George Gershwin (1898-1937) created a musical folkpiece whose language far transcends that of the Broadway theater. He had the good fortune to have as a source of his inspiration a realistic and powerful story, plus the lyrics of his brother, Ira Gershwin. Many of the songs have become the common property of the American people. The extended choral passages, based on the Negro spiritual, are among the most valuable parts of the score. They indicate with tremendous impact the mood of the piece, as well as comment on the action.

Gershwin was born of a humble Brooklyn background. During his early years his talent was expended as a pianist for publishers of popular music. The songs that he heard in the audition room provided the stimulus for his own composition of light music. Soon he became a sought-after collaborator for Broadway shows. He broke away from the confines of popular music when the bandleader Paul Whiteman commissioned him to write a work that would give jazz a place in the concert hall. The result was *Rhapsody in Blue.* At the Carnegie Hall première Gershwin himself played the piano solo. The evening brought the composer enthusiastic recognition. In the years that followed he produced a piano concerto, the witty orchestral fantasy, *An American in Paris,* and a second *Rhapsody. Porgy and Bess,* musically his richest and most individual work, appeared two years before Gershwin died in Hollywood. The cause of death was a brain tumor, discovered too late for surgical intervention.

•　　　•　　　•

Opera in 3 acts. Libretto by DuBose and Dorothy Heyward, based on the play by DuBose Heyward. *Collaborator in the lyrics:* Ira Gershwin. *Première:* Theater Guild, Boston, 1935.

Characters: Porgy, cripple (baritone); Bess (soprano); Crown (baritone); Robbins (baritone); Serena, Robbins's wife (soprano); Clara (soprano); Sporting Life (tenor); Jake (baritone); Frazier, lawyer (baritone); Maria, Lily, Strawberry Woman, Annie (sopranos and mezzo-sopranos);

The crap game in Catfish Row—Broadway production of 1935.

Mingo, Peter, Nelson, Crab Man (tenors); Jim, undertaker (baritone).

Locale: Catfish Row on the waterfront of Charleston, South Carolina. *Time:* Recent past.

•　　　•　　　•

Act I, scene 1. Catfish Row is a group of houses once inhabited by wealthy families but now the homes of poor Negroes. The curtain rises on the lively twilight activities of the Negroes: they sing, dance, and play dice. Clara sings a lullaby for her baby ("Summertime and the livin' is easy"). A quarrel arises; Crown stabs Robbins and flees. Sporting Life, a dope peddler, tries to persuade Crown's mistress Bess to run away to New York with him. She refuses, and finds shelter with Porgy, a crippled beggar confined to a goat cart.

Scene 2. Robbins's desolate widow Serena collects money for the burial of her husband. Detectives appear and try to find out Crown's whereabouts.

Act II, scene 1. It is a month later. Porgy and Bess have become strongly attached to each other. Under Porgy's influence, Bess has broken the dope habit. The Negro lawyer Frazier appears and offers to arrange a "divorce" so that Bess will be free of Crown and able to

Porgy (William Warfield) and Bess (Leesa Foster) with the

marry Porgy. The latter is delighted at the prospect of sharing the remainder of his life with Bess ("Bess, You Is My Woman Now").

Scene 2. The citizens of Catfish Row are at a picnic on Kittawah Island. The neighbors have persuaded Bess to join them while Porgy stays home alone. Suddenly Crown, who had hidden himself in a thicket, appears. Bess succumbs once more and agrees to stay with him.

Scene 3. Suffering and ill, Bess returns to Porgy several days later and begs him to protect her from Crown. A terrible hurricane breaks loose and the people in Catfish Row gather in Serena's house, where they sing and pray. Crown turns up, and mocks their fear.

Act III. The women join voices in a dirge for those who died at sea in the storm. Crown tries once more to win Bess back, but Porgy catches him trying to force his way into the house and strangles him. Detectives come to arrest Porgy for Crown's murder. While the cripple is questioned at the police station, Sporting Life persuades Bess to go to New York, where he promises her a life of pleasure and plenty. Porgy, released for lack of evidence, returns to find an empty shack. The neighbors, who tell him that Bess has gone, cannot hold him back. He calls for his cart, and starts off on the journey to seek her out in New York.

"preacher" (Eugene Brice). New York City Center production.

RIGOLETTO

Giuseppe Verdi (1813-1901) was a man deeply devoted to democratic principles; thus he was invariably attracted to subjects concerning the fight against tyranny. In *Rigoletto,* the dominant dramatic element involves resistance to the arbitrariness of a ruler. When the official censor representing the Austrian government in Venice examined 'the *Rigoletto* libretto, he immediately forbade its presentation. This happened despite the fact that Victor Hugo's original *Le Roi s'amuse* had been toned down considerably, and the title changed to the less personal *La Maledizione* (The Curse).

Nevertheless, the censor found the depiction of the ruler's sins too harsh. Accustomed to working with rapid producing, prolific composers, the Venice theater director suggested that Verdi set to music another libretto that was found acceptable for the forthcoming carnival season. The angered Verdi refused.

An unexpected stroke of luck, however, helped solve the dilemma; Venice's police chief, a man named Martello, happened to be a great music lover and an admirer of Verdi. Following his suggestions, the libretto was named after the leading character, *Rigoletto,* and France's King Francis I became the regent of an insignificant Italian state. These changes, retaining the essence of the original, achieved official sanction for the libretto. Verdi retired to Busetto, and completed the score in forty days.

During the rehearsals a remarkable thing happened; the tenor singing the Duke found an empty page in his part, and it was given him only on the day before the dress rehearsal. Verdi had realized that otherwise a musical highlight would be sung by all of music-loving Venice long before the first official performance. In this manner, the song *"La donna è mobile"* was kept secret; it turned out to be a decisive factor in the resounding success of the work. More than ever before, Verdi deepened and enriched his characterizations to a tragic degree in *Rigoletto,* his seventeenth opera. The title character himself, a jester robbed of his only joy, is a figure depicted with overwhelming musical effect.

●   ●   ●

Opera in 4 acts. Libretto by Francesco Maria Piave, based on the drama by Victor Hugo, *Le Roi s'amuse.* Première: Teatro La Fenice, Venice, 1851.

Characters: The Duke of Mantua (tenor); Rigoletto, his court jester (baritone); Gilda, his daughter (soprano);

Count Monterone (bass); Count Ceprano (baritone); Countess Ceprano, his wife (soprano); Marullo (baritone); Borsa, courtier (tenor); Giovanna, Gilda's nurse (mezzo-soprano); Sparafucile, professional assassin (bass); Maddalena, his sister (mezzo-soprano); usher (bass); page (mezzo-soprano).

Locale: Mantua and environs. *Time:* Sixteenth century.

• • •

Act I. The rise of the curtain reveals cavaliers and ladies in the festive hall of the ducal palace. In the entourage of the fast-living, pleasure-seeking Duke of Mantua is a hunchbacked jester, Rigoletto. This deformed man of dangerous character is capable of love for only one person, his pretty young daughter Gilda. His sole purpose in life is to protect her from the immoral activities of the court.

Rigoletto steps forward and makes fun of the Duke, but the Duke, maintaining his dignity, sings of his carefree existence. He tells his friend Borsa of his interest in a young girl who lives on a quiet, secluded street and grants entrance every night to a mysterious stranger. Soon the Duke mingles with the guests and turns his attention to the Countess Ceprano, one of his previous conquests. At the same time, Rigoletto mocks her jealous husband, the Count Ceprano. The latter draws his sword, but is restrained by the Duke. The old Count Monterone appears among the dancing courtiers and confronts the Duke with the accusation of having seduced his daughter. He too becomes the object of Rigoletto's mockery. Monterone responds with a curse, not only for the Duke but also for his jester.

Act II. Monterone's curse rings in the jester's ears as he makes his way home to his daughter. Rigoletto's little house adjoins the palace of Count Ceprano. Sparafucile, a professional assassin, approaches Rigoletto and offers his services. Rigoletto dismisses him and enters his house to see Gilda. When Rigoletto departs, the Duke enters the garden. He has told Gilda he is a poor student, and the girl listens happily to his declarations of love. After the Duke has departed, the courtiers appear to carry out their plan of abducting Gilda. Meeting Rigoletto, they persuade him to take part in the abduction, telling him that the victim is to be the Countess Ceprano. The courtiers bind his eyes so that he will appear to be a guiltless victim of the plot. They suppress Gilda's cries for help as she is dragged from the

house. Gradually Rigoletto becomes suspicious; he removes
his blindfold and, with horror, discovers what has happened.

Act III. Gilda has been taken to the ducal palace.
Rigoletto learns of her presence at the court, and curses
those assembled. Gilda bursts from a neighboring room
and falls into her father's arms. She admits she has suc-
cumbed to the Duke. During her confession, Monterone is
led through the hall on the way to his execution. Bitterly
he declares before a portrait of the Duke that his curse has
been ineffective. When the guards have taken Monterone
away, Rigoletto goes to the spot where the old man stood
and swears to avenge the disgrace inflicted upon both of
them.

Act IV. Rigoletto seeks out Sparafucile at his tavern
and reminds the assassin of his earlier offer. Gilda has
come with him; she declares that she will always love the
Duke, but Rigoletto wishes to give her first-hand proof of
the Duke's infidelity. The Duke appears while inside the
tavern and courts Sparafucile's sister Maddalena. Rigoletto has persuaded Gilda to disguise herself as a boy
and flee to Verona, where he will join her as soon as possible. She leaves, and Sparafucile enters. Rigoletto pays
him half the fee, saying he will come back at midnight to
take the Duke's body to the river. Maddalena, who has
fallen in love with the Duke, pleads with Sparafucile to
find another victim, and he agrees that instead of the
Duke, it shall be the first person who comes to the inn
before midnight. Gilda, now disguised, returns and, over-
hearing this, decides to become the victim herself. A thunderstorm breaks loose, and Gilda seeks entrance to the inn.
Sparafucile meets her at the door and stabs her. He places
the body in a sack, and delivers it to Rigoletto. Rigoletto
believes that his vengeance has been achieved. Suddenly he
hears the cheerful voice of the Duke.

He rips open the sack and finds that it is his own daughter. She is near death. Gilda sings a farewell, and with her
last breath, she begs her father for forgiveness. Rigoletto
cries out that the curse is fulfilled, and he collapses over
her dead body.

Der Ring

des Nibelungen

DER RING DES NIBELUNGEN

The desire of Richard Wagner (1813-1883) to construct his plots on solid literary research is best illustrated in *The Ring of the Nibelungen*. Much time and effort had to be spent before the figures of the Nibelung saga took on perspective and clarity for him before the text for the entire tetralogy was completed in 1852.

The score of *Das Rheingold* was sketched within ten weeks, and the opera was completed by the end of May, 1853. The sketches for *Walküre* were ready by the end of 1854, and the first two acts of *Siegfried* were written between the spring of 1856 and the summer of 1857. Then the composition had to be interrupted: "I have led my young Siegfried into the lonely woods, and left him there under the linden tree with a tearful farewell." Wagner stopped work on the opera not only for official reasons, but also for personal ones. He felt the need to express in music the deep beauty of his love for Mathilde Wesendonck; before he could do anything else, he had to let his soul speak—in *Tristan und Isolde*. The mighty *Ring* project was not resumed for twelve years; the comic change of pace of *Die Meistersinger von Nürnberg* had to relax the composer before he could devote himself again to the forsaken tetralogy.

Wagner's life had changed considerably during the intervening years. Above all, he had seen the fulfillment of a dream in the erection of the Bayreuth Festspielhaus (Festival Theater). The Wagner family moved to Bayreuth, and in 1872, on the composer's fifty-ninth birthday, the cornerstone of the new Festspielhaus was laid. Bayreuth also was the site of Wagner's villa, "Wahnfried" (". . . where my delusions—*Wahn*—found peace—*fried*.") The complete *Ring* had its première in Bayreuth during the summer of 1876. *Rheingold* and *Walküre* had been given previously in Munich without the composer's consent, and therefore without him present.

Although when Wagner started working on the tetralogy Siegfried was the dominant character, his importance was later succeeded by Wotan. The chief of the gods has a tragic destiny; he must witness the destruction of his own powers and hand over to mere humans the rule of the world. In Siegfried, Wagner intended to depict the ideal, perfect man. To Siegfried, material things are unimportant; for love, not ego, is his strongest motivating power. Wotan is responsible for the downfall of the gods, simply because he allows himself to be controlled by a lust for power, a lust that even permits him to make and break contracts with evil forces.

The *Ring* is filled with subtle philosophical observations and many involved subplots; its full literary impact can be appreciated only if the poetic texts are read apart from the music. Poetically, however, the *Ring* is made rather inaccessible by Wagner's constant use of a medieval German style; he is fascinated by the "Stabreim," single-verse lines which contains numerous words beginning with the same consonant.

An examination of the *Ring*'s musical language reveals a decided change in the composer's style since *Tannhäuser*. The tonal palette, which had been enriched in *Lohengrin*, had reached incredibly advanced stages of finesse in *Tristan* and *Die Meistersinger*. The new orchestral nuances may be traced in part to the use of new instruments, and in part to the individuality of Wagner's manipulation of tonal colors.

Like the music dramas that came before, the complete *Ring* is dominated by leitmotifs that signify a specific action or character. They repeat constantly in each opera, and sometimes develop with new themes as well. Of the approximately ninety themes in the *Ring,* long or short, at least a third are introduced in *Das Rheingold.*

The performance of the complete cycle represented a double triumph for Wagner. Prominent persons came from all over the world to hear *The Ring;* in addition to musicians and critics, there were many royal delegations. King Ludwig of Bavaria made an appearance, as did the German emperor Wilhelm I, who felt it his responsibility to witness so important a cultural event, even though he had no deep interest in music. The political refugee of the revolution had become the most celebrated composer in Germany.

Das

Rheingold

DAS RHEINGOLD

Music drama in 4 scenes. First performance: Munich, 1869. *Official première* as part of *The Ring:* Bayreuth, 1876.

Characters: Wotan, ruler of the gods (bass-baritone); Donner, god of thunder (baritone); Froh, god of youth, his brother (tenor); Loge, god of fire (tenor); Alberich, king of the Nibelungs (baritone); Mime, a Nibelung, and Alberich's brother (tenor); Fasolt (bass) and Fafner (bass), giants; Fricka, wife of Wotan (mezzo-soprano); Freia, sister of Fricka (soprano); Erda, goddess of wisdom (contralto); 3 Rhine-maidens, Woglinde (soprano), Wellgunde (soprano), Flosshilde (mezzo-soprano); Nibelungs, gnomes, slaves.

Locale: Bed of the Rhine, the mountains, the caverns of Nibelheim and Valhalla. *Time:* Legendary.

•　　•　　•

Scene I. The stage reveals the watery depths of the Rhine. The Rhine-maidens swim about cheerfully. Alberich, an evil-looking dwarf and leader of the Nibelung dwarfs, listens to their singing, and the maidens mock his romantic overtures. Suddenly the Rhine gold shimmers in the light of the sun. The Rhine-maidens foolishly give away the secret that whoever comes to own the gold can become the owner of the world. But there is one condition. The conqueror must forswear love. Alberich, staring at the gold, climbs to the top of the rock, grabs the prize, renounces love and steals away. The horrified Rhine-maidens utter cries of lament.

Scene II. A heavy fog sets in, then lifts disclosing a radiant mountain top. A castle can be seen in the distance, which has been built by the giants Fafner and Fasolt on commission from the gods. Wotan, ruler of the gods, and Fricka, his wife, who have been sleeping on the plateau, awaken. The god is delighted with the sight of the castle, but Fricka does not share his enthusiasm. She reproaches him for promising the giants, in return for their labors, the goddess of beauty, Freia. Freia appears and begs Wotan to protect her from the giants. The latter appear and demand their payment. Wotan claims the bargain was not a serious one. The giants are enraged, and are about to take Freia by force when Donner and Froh appear and protect her. The last to join the group is Loge, who mentions the gold Alberich has stolen from the Rhine-maidens. The giants desire the gold even more than they desire Freia; they agree to accept the Nibelung treasure instead of the goddess. But Wotan stubbornly refuses and the giants grab Freia. Loge tells Wotan that because the Goddess of Youth and Beauty has been taken away, the gods are doomed to eternal old age. Wotan then decides to take the gold from Alberich to ransom Freia, and Loge personally leads Wotan to the Nibelheim.

Scene III. Alberich has forced the Nibelung dwarfs to work as slaves in his forge. He had ordered his brother, Mime, to produce a tarnhelm, a magic helmet that can either make its wearer invisible, or permit him to assume the guise of any living being. Alberich makes himself invisible and drives Mime with a whip. Then Wotan and Loge appear and cleverly lead Alberich into boasting that he will control not only the entire world, but also the gods. Loge coaxes Alberich to disclose the secrets of the tarnhelm. First Alberich transforms himself into a gigantic worm, and then, at Loge's suggestion, into a tiny toad, whereupon they trap him. Now Wotan and Loge see their chance to take the gold; they pull the tarnhelm from the head of the helpless, transformed dwarf.

Scene IV. Wotan and Loge drag Alberich to the world of the gods, and insist on gold as the only possible condition for his release. Wotan demands the entire Nibelung treasure. Enraged, the prisoner commands his slaves to pay the ransom. The tarnhelm is part of the bargain too. Finally, Wotan insists on Alberich's golden ring as the final part of the payment. When Alberich refuses, Wotan takes it from him by force. Alberich flees, but not before he has placed a wild curse upon the ring—it shall bring destruction and death to anyone who wears it.

True to their agreement, the giants return with Freia. They demand all the gold needed to cover Freia's body from their sight. The gods pile up the treasure, but there still remains a tiny crack through which Freia's eye is visible. The giants suggest that the ring on Wotan's finger fill the crack. When Wotan refuses to give it up, the giants prepare to lead Freia off once more. Suddenly Erda emerges. She raises her voice in warning: "Give in, Wotan, give in. Escape the curse of the ring!" Wotan hurls the ring to the giants. Freia has regained her freedom, but the curse takes immediate effect. Out of greed, Fafner slays his brother. Then, victorious, Wotan and the gods start to cross a rainbow bridge to Valhalla. Just as they are about to enter Valhalla, the voices of the Rhine-maidens are heard from below, lamenting the loss of their treasure. Only Loge seems conscious of the crimes of the past; he foresees the vengeance of fate.

Die Walküre

160

DIE WALKÜRE

Opera in 3 acts. First performance: Munich, 1870. *Official première* as part of *The Ring:* Bayreuth, 1876.

Characters: Siegmund (tenor); Hunding (bass); Wotan (bass-baritone); Fricka (mezzo-soprano); Sieglinde, wife of Hunding (soprano); Brünnhilde, daughter of Wotan (soprano); 8 Valkyries, other daughters of Wotan and Erda (sopranos and mezzo-sopranos).

Locale: Hunding's hut and nearby mountain peaks.
Time: Legendary.

•   •   •

Erda's prophecy of the end of the gods has persuaded Wotan to dwell on earth. He desires to regain the ring, which Fafner guards in the guise of a gigantic worm. Wotan sires a pair of twins, Siegmund and Sieglinde, and hopes that Siegmund will be instrumental in carrying out his plan.

Act I. Siegmund seeks refuge from a storm in Hunding's hut; he has been wounded in battle. Hunding's wife Sieglinde gives the stranger water to quench his thirst. Siegmund is prepared to stagger on, maintaining that he wishes to spare the house of misfortune, but Sieglinde persuades him to stay until Hunding returns. The latter appears and realizes the youth is one of the archenemies of Hunding's clan. He is puzzled by the resemblance of the stranger and his wife. Siegmund tells of his father, whom he knows only by the name of Wälse. He speaks of the time he and his father came home from the hunt to find their home burned to the ground, the mother murdered, and no trace of the sister. Hunding is unwilling to betray the sanctity of his own hearth, but he swears to resume the battle with his enemy the next morning, far away from the hut. Sieglinde decides to save Siegmund, and adds a sleeping potion to Hunding's drink.

The unarmed Siegmund ponders how he will be able to defend himself in the coming bout. Sieglinde draws his attention to a sword lodged in the ash tree in the center of the hut. She explains that on the day of her wedding it was rammed into the tree by a mysterious stranger. It is intended for the man who can draw it from the tree and free Sieglinde from her marriage with Hunding, which she was forced into. Sieglinde has learned from Siegmund's narrative that he is her twin brother, and the man destined to save her from Hunding. Filled with ecstasy at this realization, Siegmund succeeds in pulling the sword from the tree. He utters a mighty cry: "You must be both bride and sister to me—thus may the Wälsung blood continue to flourish." They passionately embrace and leave together.

Act II. Wotan instructs his favorite daughter, the warrior-maiden Brünnhilde, to allow Siegmund to emerge victorious in his battle with Hunding. Brünnhilde departs, amid lusty battle cries. Fricka, the goddess of marriage, appears, and demands that Wotan punish the incestuous pair, Siegmund and Sieglinde. Wotan protests, but later commands Siegmund's death. Brünnhilde returns, and is told of her father's fate: his belief that Siegmund could save the gods was self-deception. Wotan tells her of his attempts to regain the ring. Wotan says he longs for the end. The one who will bring about this end, he believes, is Alberich who has used the power of the Nibelungen gold to force a woman to bear him a son, who will avenge him.

Siegmund and Sieglinde appear, and rest from their flight. Brünnhilde tells Siegmund he is to lose the coming battle with Hunding. Siegmund is determined to die only with Sieglinde, and that they must never be parted. Such love moves Brünnhilde; disobeying Wotan's command, she promises to make Siegmund the victor. Hunding appears. When the fight starts, Brünnhilde places herself at Siegmund's side. Just as Siegmund is about to strike Hunding with the fatal blow, Wotan appears between the two men. He smashes Siegmund's sword with his spear. Now the young warrior is helpless, and Hunding plunges his spear into his enemy's breast. Brünnhilde rushes off with Sieglinde. A disdainful gesture from Wotan causes Hunding, too, to fall lifeless to the ground. Wotan vows to punish Brünnhilde.

Act III. Spirited battle cries accompany the Valkyrie maidens as they bring the bodies of fallen heroes to Valhalla. Brünnhilde is the last to appear. The maidens are surprised to see her carrying, instead of a warrior, the feverish Sieglinde. Sieglinde expects a child, and hopes to live at least until its birth. Brünnhilde gives her the pieces of Siegmund's sword, and makes the prophecy that her son will be the world's mightiest hero. For his sake Sieglinde must endure all dangers. Sieglinde then leaves.

Wotan appears, enraged over his daughter's disrespect for his command. His punishment is stern; she is to be stripped of all godly attributes and put into a trance-like sleep. Brünnhilde begs her father for mercy. Eventually Wotan relents to the extent that he agrees to surround the sleeping Brünnhilde with a protective magic fire. She can be awakened only by a fearless hero who dares penetrate the flames. With tender words and a last kiss, Wotan puts his daughter to sleep.

Siegfried

SIEGFRIED

Opera in 3 acts. Première: Festspielhaus, Bayreuth, 1876.
Characters: Siegfried (tenor); Mime (tenor); Wanderer, Wotan in disguise (bass-baritone); Alberich (baritone); Fafner (bass); Erda (contralto); Brünnhilde (soprano); voice of the forest bird (soprano).
Locale: A forge in the woods, the forest near Fafner's cave, mountain areas. *Time:* Legendary.

• • •

Act I. The setting discloses a thick forest near the cave in which Fafner, transformed into a gigantic worm, guards the Nibelungs' gold. Mime tries unsuccessfully to forge a weapon. Sieglinde has borne her son in Mime's cave, and before her death she gave the dwarf the remains of Siegmund's sword. Sieglinde's child, Siegfried, has since grown into a powerful, unruly youth. Mime hopes to use Siegfried to force Fafner to give up the treasure.

Siegfried's appearance is announced by a bold horn call. The youth examines Mime's work with scorn and hurls it at his feet. When the fearful Mime makes excuses for his clumsy craftsmanship, Siegfried demands to know more about his own background. The youth listens, deeply moved, to the story of his parents' fate. To prove his story, Mime produces the pieces of Siegmund's sword. Siegfried commands the dwarf to forge him a new sword, using these pieces. Mime falls into deep brooding, for he doubts his ability to produce the weapon. He is surprised by the appearance of the Wanderer (in this disguise, Wotan makes his way through the world—he has lost both his desire for power and his need for activity).

Wotan engages Mime in a game of riddles, and agrees to die if he cannot answer three of Mime's questions. First Mime asks the name of those who dwell far below the earth. Answer: The Nibelungen. The second question concerns those who live on earth. Answer: The giants. The final query asks who lives in the cloudy heights. Answer: The gods in Valhalla. By responding correctly all three times, the Wanderer has saved his life. Now it is his turn to ask Mime three questions. First he asks the name of the race that Wotan loves the most, yet treats very badly. Answer: The Wälsungen, who produced Siegmund and Sieglinde. The second question: What is the sword called with which Siegfried could kill Fafner? Answer: Nothung, a sword now in fragments which Wotan once drove into an ash tree. Mime falters only on the third question: Who will succeed in reforging the sword? The Wanderer answers for him: "Only he who never knew fear can forge Nothung once more." The Wanderer spares the frightened Mime's life.

Siegfried returns, and sets to work at the forge himself. Mime watches, and soon realizes that Siegfried is succeeding in the task; he decides to give the youth a magic potion that will enable Mime to regain control of the sword. The sword complete, Siegfried strikes a mighty blow on the anvil. It falls apart, neatly cut in half. Mime is terrified.

Act II. Alberich stands guard in a deep forest near the cave in which Fafner, transformed into a gigantic dragon, hoards his treasure. Alberich recognizes Wotan approaching in the form of the Wanderer, and tries to drive him away with verbal abuse. Wotan insists that he is no longer interested in owning the gold. In fact, he even awakens the sleeping Fafner to warn him of the impending arrival of Siegfried and Mime. Alberich offers to help protect Fafner in return for the ring. Fafner, however, does not wish to be disturbed; yawning, he replies, "I lie here, and I maintain my possessions—let me sleep!" The Wanderer departs, laughing at Alberich's unsuccessful plotting. The Nibelung replies with a warning about the impending downfall of the gods.

Dawn breaks. Siegfried and Mime stop to rest. They have arrived at the spot where Siegfried supposedly will "learn now to be afraid." Siegfried is intent on fighting the monster, and advises Mime to seek shelter at a distance. When the dwarf goes off, Siegfried is lost in revery, overcome with the beauty of the forest. He carves a crude flute from a branch, and makes an unsuccessful effort to imitate the song of the birds. Then he produces some more powerful tones on his horn. The sounds awaken the gigantic dragon, who thrashes about discontentedly. Siegfried plunges his sword into the monster's heart. The dying Fafner warns him about the curse of the gold. When Siegfried withdraws his sword, a drop of blood falls on his hand. Instinctively, he puts it to his mouth. Tasting the dragon's blood has imbued the youth with a new magical power; now he can understand the language of the birds. A forest bird tells Siegfried where the treasure is hidden. Siegfried explores Fafner's cave and finds the tarnhelm—the magic helmet—and the ring. Mime and Alberich, both of whom want to profit from the slaying of the dragon, meet at the entrance to the cave. The brothers fight jealously over the gold they do not yet possess. Siegfried returns with his prizes. Once again he listens to the bird, who warns him of Mime's greed. When the dwarf offers him the magic potion, Siegfried strikes him with his sword and throws the body into the cave. The dead dragon is left to seal the entrance. Suddenly finding himself alone, Siegfried is filled with a strange longing. The song of the wood bird leads him to the rocky cliffs where Brünnhilde is sleeping.

Act III, scene 1. Because he is in possession of the ring, Siegfried is in a position to rule the world. Wotan, still disguised as the Wanderer, awakens Erda to learn more of the fate of the world. Wotan does not fear the downfall of the gods, but instead suspects that the hero who will awaken Brünnhilde will be the heir to his power. Erda goes back to her unearthly sleep in the shadowy darkness.

Scene 2. Led on by the forest bird, Siegfried meets the Wanderer on his journey toward the Valkyrie's rock. When Siegfried answers his questions with haughty boldness, the god is angered. He blocks Siegfried's path toward Brünnhilde's resting place. To the Wanderer's question about where he got the sword, Siegfried replies that he made it himself. These questions, and the old man's missing eye,

Siegfried's kiss awakens Brünnhilde after she had a long sleep

convince Siegfried that he has come face to face with the man responsible for his father's (Siegmund's) death. He draws his sword, and, with one mighty blow, reduces Wotan's spear to splinters. Only then the god realizes that his powers are at an end forever, and that he is unable to stop the young hero from penetrating the flames that surround Brünnhilde. With an exuberant horn call and the lusty cry, "To find my bride amid the flames," Siegfried rushes off to the fiery heights.

Scene 3. Siegfried comes upon Brünnhilde sleeping beneath a fir tree at the sunny peak of a rocky cliff. Never having seen a maiden before, he stands before the sleeping form, spellbound. Carefully, he loosens her shining armor and kisses her ardently. Brünnhilde opens her eyes slowly, raises herself, and greets the sun ecstatically. She recognizes the youth as the son of the woman she once protected. She realizes that her awakening signifies that she has lost her godhood, and is now a mortal; love has transformed her into a human being, and she guesses that the destruction of the gods is imminent. She finds a new fulfillment in her coming union: "Shining love, and laughing death!"

cast by the spell of Wotan. Bayreuth Festival production, 1952.

Götterdämmerung

GÖTTERDÄMMERUNG

Music drama in a prologue and 3 acts. Première: Fest-spielhaus, Bayreuth, 1876.

Characters: Siegfried (tenor); Gunther, King of the Gibichung (baritone); Hagen, his half-brother (bass); Alberich (bass); Brünnhilde (soprano); Gutrune, sister of Gunther (soprano); Waltraute, a Valkyrie (mezzo-soprano); 3 Norns (contralto, mezzo-soprano, soprano); 3 Rhine-maidens (2 sopranos, 1 mezzo-soprano).

Locale: The Valkyries' rock, hall of the Gibichungs, banks of the Rhine near Gunther's castle, valley in the rocky forest. *Time:* Legendary.

• • •

Prologue. It is night. The Norns, daughters of Erda, spin the rope of life. The ash tree of the world, which used to anchor the rope, has died. A fir tree now stands in its place. The second Norn has chosen a sharp cliff edge to which she fastens the end of her rope. The third Norn throws the end of the rope back to each of her sisters. The Norns tell of how Wotan gave up one eye in return for a drink from the well of wisdom, and how Siegfried smashed both Wotan's spear and the power it held. The twigs of the ash tree, which are piled up around Valhalla, will burn and the flames will consume both the castle and its inhabitants. To the horror of the Norns, the rope breaks. Lamenting their fate, they disappear.

At dawn Siegfried and Brünnhilde ascend a cliff and express their passionate love. Spurred to new deeds of heroism, Siegfried plans to go into the world. As a symbol of his devotion, he gives his bride the ring of the Nibelungen. In return, Brünnhilde gives him her steed, Grane.

Act I. After a long orchestral Prelude that depicts Siegfried's journey along the Rhine, the curtain rises on the hall of the Gibichung Castle. Gunther, Gutrune, and Hagen are seated at a table. Hagen advises both brother and sister to get married; for Gunther he suggests Brünnhilde. Siegfried has gained possession of the Nibelungs' gold, which assures him world power. Hagen hopes to interest Siegfried in Gutrune, and thus get the gold himself. He has a magic potion that will make Siegfried forget his past, including his love for Brünnhilde.

Siegfried's horn is heard in the distance. Hagen summons the hero, and invites him to spend some time with the Gibichungs. As proof of her hospitality, Gutrune offers Siegfried a drink, the magic potion. All memories of Brünnhilde fade immediately, and Siegfried is filled with passionate longing for Gutrune. When Gunther promises him Gutrune's hand, Siegfried agrees to force Brünnhilde to come to the castle as Gunther's bride. Gunther and Siegfried prick their arms with their swords and mix their blood with wine; raising their goblets, they drink a blood oath confirming their undying friendship. Siegfried, who in the guise of Gunther, will carry out the abduction of Brünnhilde, departs with his new blood-brother. Hagen stays behind, filled with hope that his intrigue will put him in possession of Brünnhilde's ring.

Lost in reverie, Brünnhilde gazes lovingly at the ring Siegfried gave her. Her sister, the Valkyrie Waltraute, appears, and begs her to give the ring back to its rightful owners, the Rhine-maidens. Only thus will the gods be freed of the curse connected with the ring. But Brünnhilde is unwilling to part with Siegfried's symbolic gift. Siegfried appears, transformed by the tarnhelm into Gunther's form. He declares his desire to marry her, and despite her mighty resistance, forces the ring from her.

Act II. Alberich appears out of the darkness. He wants to convince Hagen, his son, of the importance of regaining the golden ring taken from him. Siegfried and Gunther enter, accompanied by the humiliated, disconsolate Brünnhilde. Hagen summons his men so that the populace may know of Gunther's chosen bride. Brünnhilde catches sight of Siegfried at Gutrune's side. When she sees the golden ring on his finger, she realizes she has been made the victim of a horrible conspiracy. She guesses that it was Siegfried who took the ring from her in the guise of Gunther. In a fit of rage, she makes her accusation. Still under the influence of the magic drink, Siegfried denies his guilt, and invites all present to join in the wedding feast to celebrate his betrothal to Gutrune. Overcome with the desire for revenge, Brünnhilde gives away the secret of Siegfried's super-human power. He can be wounded only at one small spot between his shoulder blades, and this is meaningless for the hero never retreats from battles showing his back to the enemy. Hagen plans to strike the hated Siegfried in his one mortal spot. Gunther hesitates a long time before agreeing to participate in the murder; he does not wish to break his bond of brotherhood with Siegfried, nor does he want to deprive his sister of her husband. Finally he joins Brünnhilde and Hagen in a new oath: "Thus it must be, Siegfried must fall!"

Act III. The Rhine-maidens emerge from the waves to beg the sun to send them a hero who can restore to them the stolen ring. First with flattery, then with threats, they try to persuade Siegfried to help them. When they realize he is unwilling, they prophesy the misfortune that the ring will bring its wearer. Then they return to the depths of the Rhine. Gunther appears with Hagen and his men. Laughingly, Siegfried admits that his hunting has been unsuccessful. Hagen asks Siegfried to tell of his earlier life. Siegfried tells of his youth with Mime, who taught him how to forge a sword, and how he slew the dragon Fafner. Hagen offers Siegfried a drink from his horn, which contains a potion that will restore the hero's memory. Siegfried betrays the fact that he bears a passionate love for his bride, Brünnhilde. At this moment, two ravens circle above Siegfried. "What are they whispering?" Hagen asks. Just as Siegfried turns to watch the flight of the birds, Hagen's spear strikes the unprotected spot on his back. The wounded Siegfried tries to crush Hagen with his shield, but falls powerless to the ground. The dying Siegfried thinks of Brünnhilde. As the powerful funeral music rises from the orchestra, the men carry the body off.

Hagen nears the Gibichung hall with the gruesome reward of the hunt, the dead Siegfried. In response to Gutrune's accusations, Gunther exposes Hagen as the murderer. When Gunther refuses to let Hagen have the ring, the latter slays his half-brother. Once again the curse has taken its toll. Now Hagen steps forward to seize the ring from Siegfried's finger. An unearthly power enables the dead hero to raise his hand in warning. Everyone is horrorstruck. Brünnhilde steps forward and confirms the invalidity of Gutrune's marriage. She commands a funeral pyre to be erected along the shore of the Rhine, and Siegfried's body to be placed upon it. She draws the ring from Siegfried's finger and places it on her own hand, lights the fire, and on her steed Grane springs into the flames. The waters of the Rhine swell, and the Rhine-maidens emerge to take the ring from Brünnhilde's lifeless hand. The gold has been returned to its rightful owners, and will no longer carry the curse. Hagen, who had hoped still to regain the ring, is dragged by the Rhine-maidens to the depths of the river. The funeral fire spreads until the Gibichung hall is consumed. In the distance, Valhalla, the castle of the gods, is also seen aflame. The curse of the ring has been fulfilled.

Siegfried (Hans Hopf) leaves Brünnhilde (Birgit Nilsson) for the world of the Gibichung. Bayreuth Festival, 1960.

Der

Rosenkavalier

DER ROSENKAVALIER

After *Salome* and *Elektra,* both of which are dominated by hate and a passionate wish for annihilation, Richard Strauss (1864-1949) felt the need for spiritual relaxation. Together with Hugo von Hofmannsthal, he hit upon the idea of writing an opera, *Semiramis,* to be based upon Calderon's *Die Tochter der Luft.* Plans for a comic opera, *Casanova,* were also under discussion. Finally the librettist suggested a light opera that was to have a Viennese atmosphere and bear the temporary title *Ochs.* The composer offered wide-ranging suggestions concerning the action and the dialogue. He wanted to elicit laughter from his audience, not smiles and chuckles: "What I miss in our work so far is a truly comic situation." Strauss requested that certain lines be added; he pointed out possibilities of heightened dramatic effect. The composer followed the work of his librettist with feverish creative energy.

The reception accorded *Der Rosenkavalier* at its Dresden première in 1911 was enthusiastic. To the present day, it has remained Strauss's most popular stage work.

Strauss commanded here such richness of imagination, such melodic beauty, and such finesse of characterization, that it is no exaggeration to claim that this score is the most artistic and dramatically effective comedy in all modern opera. The love scene between the Marschallin and her young suitor, the lusty entrance of the crude Baron Ochs von Lerchenau, and the complex ensembles of the scene in the Princess's boudoir all bear out that claim.

•   •   •

Comedy with music, in 3 acts. Libretto by Hugo von Hofmannsthal.

Première: Hofoper, Dresden, 1911.

Characters: The Marschallin, Princess of Werdenberg (soprano); Baron Ochs von Lerchenau (bass); Octavian, young nobleman (soprano or mezzo-soprano); Herr von Faninal, rich merchant who has just become a nobleman (baritone); Sophie, his daughter (soprano); Marianne, Faninal's housekeeper (soprano); Valzacchi, intriguer (tenor); Annina, his partner (contralto); Police Commissioner (bass); the Marschallin's major-domo (tenor); Faninal's major-domo (tenor); Italian singer (tenor); notary (bass); innkeeper (tenor); 3 noble orphans (1 soprano, 2 mezzo-sopranos); milliner, animal vendor, footmen, Negro servant, waiters, flutist, hairdresser, messengers, kitchen staff, doctor, etc.

Locale: Vienna. *Time:* Reign of Maria Theresa (1740-80).

•   •   •

Act I. In the royal bedchamber, Octavian kneels at the Marschallin's bedside. A little Negro servant brings breakfast. The Marschallin is frightened by a noise in the anteroom, and fears that her husband has come home prematurely from his hunting trip. Octavian hides. The intruder turns out to be the Marschallin's crude country cousin, Baron Ochs von Lerchenau, who rudely demands admittance. Octavian has hastily donned a maid's clothes, and the Marschallin goes along with the masquerade, calling him "Mariandel." Ochs loses no time in pressing amorous attentions on "Mariandel." Ochs tells the Marschallin of his intentions to marry the young daughter of the *nouveau riche* Herr von Faninal. He needs someone to present the symbolic silver rose to his fiancée at the traditional first visit to her family. In a mischievous mood, the Marschallin recommends Octavian, whose portrait she shows her cousin in a locket.

Still playing the role of maid, Octavian grants admission to a number of people waiting in an anteroom to see the Marschallin. Led by their mother, three noble orphans beg for financial aid; an animal vendor parades his little dogs; a milliner shows her newest creations; an Italian tenor offers a passionate aria for the Marschallin's pleasure. Ochs is deeply engaged in an argument with a notary concerning his bride-to-be's dowry. One of his lackeys brings the silver rose. The spy Valzacchi and his partner Annina offer their shady services to Ochs.

Everyone departs, leaving the Marschallin alone and deep in thought. Gazing at herself in the mirror while her hair was being dressed, she suddenly had realized the nearness of old age. When Octavian returns, she tells him that sooner or later he will forsake her for a younger and prettier woman. After he has departed, the Marschallin notices that he has forgotten to take the casket containing the silver rose. The little Negro servant is dispatched to take it to him. The Marschallin resumes her painful contemplation.

Act II. Sophie awaits the arrival of the messenger with the rose in the festive hall of Faninal's chateau. After Octavian presents the rose, Sophie and he are drawn to each other and engage in conversation. Ochs appears and approaches the young girl with a bold intimacy that frightens her. Soon, however, he retires to another room with the girl's father to discuss further details of the marriage contract. Sophie is horrified at the prospect of having to marry this uncouth man. In desperation she turns to Octavian for help. Valzacchi and Annina have overheard the affectionate pair, and now summon Ochs, their employer. Octavian calls him a dowry hunter. This prompts Ochs to draw his sword, but he drops it when Octavian inflicts a tiny scratch on his arm. In response to Ochs's wild cries, Faninal's entire household staff scrambles to the scene, as does Ochs's seedy peasant entourage. Faninal sends Sophie to her room and unceremoniously dismisses Octavian. Meanwhile, Ochs has recovered from his fright. His mood is improved further when Annina brings him a note from "Mariandel" informing him of "her" availability the next night. He retires to another room to dictate an answer.

Act III. In an inn at the outskirts of the city, Ochs has reserved a private room for his rendezvous. Octavian has employed Valzacchi and Annina in his plot to dupe the baron. Five disreputable-looking guests have been hidden in various parts of the room, and are instructed to interrupt the projected meeting upon a given signal.

The baron enters with "Mariandel." Just as he is about to kiss her, he notices her striking resemblance to Octavian. The first interruption is made by Annina, who bursts into the room with crying children in tow and claims to be Ochs's wife. Panels open at various places on the wall and reveal suspicious-looking faces. Unnerved, the baron calls the police. The Police Commissioner appears, and Ochs tries to pass off "Mariandel" as his fiancée Sophie. Faninal is summoned and is outraged at Ochs's false claim. Sophie, who had been waiting outside in a carriage, enters to repudiate further the baron's protestations. "Mariandel" whispers something to the Commissioner and disappears behind the curtain of an alcove. Piece by piece, "Mariandel's" clothing is thrown into the room. The Marschallin enters, and explains it was all a farce.

Octavian emerges from the alcove dressed as a man again. The Marschallin advises Ochs to retreat gracefully. She watches the young couple together, and acknowledges that their love is about to bloom. A few sad words mark her renunciation. She leaves the room and Octavian and Sophie declare their love to each other. Once more, the Marschallin enters, this time with Faninal; they indicate their approval. Octavian and Sophie embrace and rush out. The little Negro servant is sent back to retrieve a handkerchief dropped by Sophie. After a brief search, he finds it, and dashes out to the waiting carriage.

Sophie (Anneliese Rothenberger) is horrified at the advances of Baron Ochs (Otto Edelman). Metropolitan Opera production.

ALOME

SALOME

Still under the influence of Wagner, Richard Strauss (1864-1949) wrote the full-length opera *Guntram* in 1894. The work had a lukewarm reception because of the distinctly derivative nature of both words and music. *Feuersnot* (Fire Famine), containing some rather satirical references to the narrow-mindedness of Strauss's native Munich, proved more successful. Four years after the Dresden première of that second opera, *Salome* (1905) was presented in the same city. With *Salome,* Strauss became the center of attention throughout the world of music. The composer used for his libretto a literal translation of Oscar Wilde's, without any of the alterations usual in transforming a play to the opera stage. Thus the startling effectiveness of the original script was retained.

Freeing himself completely from the confines of Wagner's tonal language, Strauss developed his own style in *Salome*. To a great extent he abandoned traditional harmonic structures. The vocal lines move in the exaggerated contours of highly complex recitatives; the orchestra overflows with striking dissonances and unexpected chord connections. Nevertheless, the composer still finds sufficient room for broad, romantic melodies.

The work was acclaimed in avant-garde circles because of its clever manipulation of the Biblical subject and its

Salome (Elaine Malbin, left) confronts Herod (Andrew Mc-

pioneering excursion into new musical realms. The conservative segment of the public, however, rejected the work.

• • •

Music drama in 1 act. Libretto: play by Oscar Wilde, in German translation by Hedwig Lachmann. *Première:* Court Opera, Dresden, 1905.

Characters: Herod, Tetrarch of Judea (tenor); Herodias, his wife (mezzo-soprano); Salome, her daughter (soprano); Jokanaan, the prophet John the Baptist (baritone); Narraboth, captain of the guards (tenor); page of Herodias (mezzo-soprano); 5 Jews (4 tenors, 1 bass); 2 Nazarenes (tenor, bass); slave, Cappadocian, executioner, soldiers.

Locale: Terrace at the palace of Herod. *Time:* About A.D. 30.

• • •

The moon illuminates the terrace from which Narraboth, the captain of the guard, watches Salome at a banquet in the great hall. He is filled with desire for her. The guards speak of the prophet Jokanaan, who is being held captive in the cistern of the terrace. Suddenly the prophet's voice is heard from below foretelling the coming of Christ. Salome, no longer able to stand the lecherous glances of her stepfather Herod, comes onto the terrace and hears the words

Kinley) as Herodias (Lorna Sidney) listens. NBC TV Opera.

of prophecy. Yielding to her command, Narraboth disregards Herod's orders and opens the cistern. Jokanaan emerges and voices his condemnation of Herod and Herodias. Salome is fascinated by him and gripped with sensual longing; she tries to touch his body, and as he turns from her in scorn she attempts to kiss his lips. "Never, daughter of Sodom, never!" he cries. Narraboth can stand no more of Salome's eroticism; he plunges his sword into his own breast. Without so much as a glance at the dead captain, the obsessed woman repeats her plea: "Let me kiss your mouth, Jokanaan!" Damning her, Jokanaan descends once more to his dungeon. Salome ponders her revenge.

Herod, Herodias, and their party come onto the terrace. Herod slips in the blood of Narraboth, and he is overcome with horror and deep foreboding. Seeing Salome cowering near the cistern, he invites her to share his wine and fruit. Salome coldly refuses.

The voice of Jokanaan rises again. Despite Herodias's entreaties, Herod does not dare silence the prophet forever, for Herod sees in him the qualities of a holy man who has witnessed the face of God. This precipitates a noisy dispute among five Jews acting as delegates of their people at the court. Two Nazarenes speak of the wonders performed by Jesus, telling Herod that He has awakened the dead. To distract himself from such disturbing thoughts, Herod begs Salome to dance, offering her the fulfillment of any wish in return. In spite of the protests of Herodias, Salome dances, discarding one by one the seven veils that cloak her beautiful body.

At the end of the dance, Herod asks what she wishes as a reward, and she demands the head of Jokanaan on a silver platter. Herod is revolted and offers instead the most prized objects in his possession, even the sacred veil of the temple. Coldly, Salome insists on her one demand. Herodias removes the ring of death from the finger of her weak-willed husband and hands it to the executioner. The executioner, carrying his mighty sword, descends into the cistern.

In terrifying silence, all wait. Finally the executioner appears, with the head of Jokanaan on a platter. Salome holds the platter in her hands, and gazes for a long time at the head: "If you had only looked at me, you would have loved me. The secret of love is greater than the secret of death." Horrified, Herod commands: "Kill that woman!" The guards surround Salome and crush her with their shields.

[]

Herod (Andrew McKinley) is horrified at Salome's demand for the head of the Baptist. But Herodias (Lorna Sidney) encourages the demand until Herod gives in. NBC TV Opera.

TANNHÄUSER

As early as 1841, when he was living in Paris, Richard Wagner (1813-1883) was occupied with plans inspired by a book of legends for an opera called *Der Venusberg*. After his return to Germany, he was spending the summer near Teplitz, and on a walk the beauty of nature and the silence of the moonlit night so excited his imagination that he immediately sketched the outline of a poem. Wagner combined two different themes: the singing tournaments, which took place around the year 1200, and the later story of Tannhäuser. He interwove still other themes from old German legends with the two basic plots. The composer completed the rough draft of the music in less than four months. That same year, 1845, the première took place under the composer's direction at the Dresden Court Opera, where Wagner was Kapellmeister.

No work of Wagner's was revised as many times as *Tannhäuser*. The most important alterations were made in the Paris production of 1861. Wagner opposed with stubborn resistance the demand of the opera management to insert the customary ballet in the second act. He was finally ready to compromise by expanding the somewhat tame scene in the Venusberg with voluptuous dancing. Thus the so-called "Paris version" originated.

Tannhäuser is important as a transitional link in Wagner's music dramas. To a large extent, the opera still follows the stylistic characteristics of traditional grand opera, mingled with the melodic and harmonic intricacies of his later creations. Tannhäuser's "Rome Narrative," for example, with its highly intensified pathos contrasts strongly with Wolfram's "Evening Star" aria, which contains the expressive, songlike elements of Italian opera. The dichotomy between the sensuous orgy in the Venusberg and the pilgrims' journey to Rome gives the overture a heightened spiritual significance.

Elizabeth's entrance, "Dich, teure Halle, gruess ich Wieder," Tannhäuser's stormy confession in honor of Venus and the shocked repulsion of all present, Elizabeth's prayer, "Allmaechtige Jungfrau," in the third act, are but a few of the scenes that even today retain their singularly impressive power.

• • •

Opera in 3 acts. Première: Dresden, 1845.
Characters: Hermann, Landgrave of Thuringia (bass); Tannhäuser (tenor); Wolfram von Eschenbach (baritone);

Walther von der Vogelweide (tenor); Heinrich, the scribe (tenor); Reimar von Zweter (bass); Elizabeth, niece of the Landgrave (soprano); Venus (soprano or mezzo-soprano); shepherd boy (soprano); 4 pages; minstrel knights.

Locale: In and near Wartburg Castle, Thuringia, Germany. *Time:* Early thirteenth century.

• • •

Act I, scene 1. In a deep grotto of the Venusberg, the Goddess of Love is holding a sensuous feast, with bacchantes, bacchants, sirens, and nymphs. Tannhäuser, subdued by the Goddess of Love's magic, lies at her feet. He pays homage to her in a turbulent song, imploring her to set him free. Venus tries to rebuff him with threats, but his drive toward freedom is indomitable. At his cry: "My strength lies in Mary!" Venus sinks down with a shriek, and the whole magical world disappears.

Scene 2. The scene is a valley near the Wartburg in the springtime. The song of a shepherd is heard. Devout pilgrims, en route to Rome to seek pardon for their sins, pass by. Tannhäuser kneels in prayer before a statue of Mary. He is startled by the Landgrave and his retainers, returning from the hunt. All joyfully greet their long-departed friend and beg him to join them. When Wolfram alludes to the constant love of Elizabeth for Tannhäuser, the latter declares: "Oh, lead me to her."

Act II. Elizabeth, who has retired from all festivities since the disappearance of Tannhäuser, decides to attend the impending minstrel competition. She enters the hall in a state of excitement. Tannhäuser appears, and throws himself at her feet. She bids him rise, for this place is his kingdom. After Tannhäuser has left, the Landgrave appears and assures her that her longing will soon be satisfied.

The lords and ladies enter the hall in solemn procession, and the singers in the contest take their places in the foreground. The Landgrave first explains the basic purpose of the contest: to define the nature of love. Elizabeth will award the victor a prize "as grand and rich" as he may desire. Wolfram is chosen to be the first contestant. He describes pure adoration as the innermost nature of love. After Walther von der Vogelweide has expressed similar sentiments, Tannhäuser rises, and in an ecstatic hymn praises sensual love. Bitter discussion and argument follow. Tannhäuser interrupts with uninhibited praise of the delights of Venus. Indignantly the ladies, except Elizabeth, leave their seats, while the knights rush at the blasphemer, brandishing their weapons. Tannhäuser throws himself at Elizabeth's feet. She implores pardon for the sinner, bewitched by the Goddess of Love. The wretched Tannhäuser takes the Landgrave's advice to join the pilgrims, and to seek forgiveness from the Pope. The act ends with Tannhäuser's cry: "To Rome!" echoed by the assemblage.

Act III. It is spring again. Wolfram contemplates Elizabeth, who is praying before an image of Mary. Vainly, she looks for Tannhäuser among the passing pilgrims. She prays for his salvation. Refusing Wolfram's offer to accompany her, she returns to the castle alone. Wolfram, thinking of Elizabeth, sings to the evening star shining in the heavens. The song is heard by Tannhäuser, who has returned from his pilgrimage without having obtained the absolution of the Pope. His sojourn in the Venusberg

The Landgrave (Joseph Greindl) welcomes the minstrel knights

makes redemption impossible—as impossible as the budding of the Pope's staff. He acknowledges with despair that the only thing he can do is return to the kingdom of Venus.

The Goddess of Love appears and tries to lure Tannhäuser into her entourage. He tries to free himself from Wolfram, who tries to restrain him. Suddenly the magic vision sinks into the ground. Led by the Landgrave, the knights approach with Elizabeth's coffin. Crying out, "St. Elizabeth, pray for me!" Tannhäuser falls dead on the bier. The pilgrims are overcome by the miracle that takes place before their eyes: The Pope's staff has budded with green leaves. They proclaim that God's mercy through the sacrificial death of Elizabeth has lifted the curse from Tannhäuser and brought him the peace of the blessed.

Everyone hails the miracle by which Tannhäuser's redemption is assured.

to the magnificent hall of song. Bayreuth Festival of 1954.

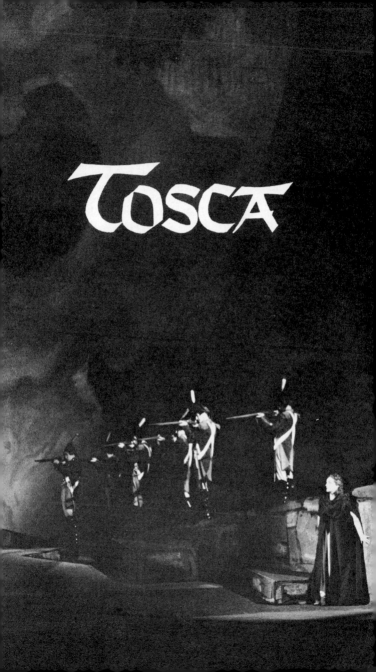

TOSCA

It was the great tragic actress Sarah Bernhardt who stimulated Giacomo Puccini (1858-1924) to feeling that a libretto should be adapted from the Sardou play, *La Tosca*. The composer was immediately struck by its dramatic power, but he questioned his own competence to set this stirring drama to music. It was some years later that Puccini received Illica's completed libretto, through a remarkable set of circumstances. Illica had prepared the book for the composer Alberto Franchetti. Illica and the publisher Ricordi, however, persuaded Franchetti that the opera would not suit his talents, and with the libretto thus available, Ricordi went to Puccini and triumphantly produced the manuscript. Just then church bells began to ring. "There you already have the opera's prelude," Ricordi said.

For a place to work, Puccini chose Chiatri, an out-of-the-way little place near Torre del Lago. A piano was ordered, for Puccini was accustomed to composing at the keyboard. He demanded certain revisions in the libretto, and he himself made some additions, including the scene between the sacristan and the mischievous choir boys, Cavaradossi's love song in the third act, and the ceremony that takes place during the *Te Deum* of Act I.

Unknown persons organized a disruptive claque that caused some unrest during the *Tosca* première. Neither this nor the mixed reception by the Italian press diminished the public's approval. Puccini reached an artistic standard even higher than in *La Bohème*. Here, he no longer paints people and situations with the light touch of a pastel artist; rather, he develops solid character and action with far bolder strokes. The intellectual duel between Tosca and the devilish Scarpia, with its tragic end, is one of the most stimulating scenes in all of Italy's *verismo* opera.

• • •

Opera in 3 acts. Libretto by Luigi Illica and Giuseppe Giacosa, based on the play by Victorien Sardou. *Première:* Rome, 1900.

Characters: Floria Tosca, famous singer (soprano); Mario Cavaradossi, painter (tenor); Baron Scarpia, chief of police in Rome (baritone); Cesare Angelotti, escaped political prisoner (bass); Spoletta, police agent (tenor); sacristan (baritone or bass); police officer (bass); jailer (bass); shepherd boy (contralto).

Locale: Rome. *Time:* 1800.

• • •

Act I. Cesare Angelotti, once Consul of Rome and now a political prisoner, has escaped and seeks asylum in the church of Sant' Andrea della Valle. He hears the footsteps of the sacristan and hides. The painter Mario Cavaradossi enters to work on a picture. The features of the woman Cavaradossi is painting bear a strong resemblance to a certain beauty who appears in the church frequently to pray. When the sacristan departs, Angelotti comes out of hiding. Cavaradossi recognizes him, locks the door, and gives the starving fugitive his own basket of food. When a woman's voice is heard, Angelotti hides again and Cavaradossi opens the door. Tosca appears. Jealously she studies the portrait, disturbed by the fact that the subject is blonde, whereas she herself is brunette. She is in love with the painter, and arranges a rendezvous with him. After her departure, Angelotti returns and tells Cavaradossi that his sister, who is the model for the portrait, has hidden clothing for him behind the altar. Cavaradossi decides to hide the fugitive in his villa.

The sacristan enters with a group of choristers, and tells Cavaradossi that a High Mass is to be celebrated in honor of a victory over Napoleon. Suddenly Scarpia, the chief of police, enters to conduct personally the search for the escaped prisoner. He finds a fan belonging to Angelotti's sister, and sees the portrait bearing her likeness. Tosca returns. Her suspicions are further aroused by the fan Scarpia shows her. She rushes off, expecting to surprise her supposed rival in Cavaradossi's house. Scarpia has his secret agents follow her. The church fills with worshipers. A cardinal appears in his crimson robes, surrounded by priests and choristers. The *Te Deum,* reinforced by a mighty organ, resounds in the church.

Act II. Scarpia is dining in his chambers at the Palazzo Farnese, listening from the distance to Tosca sing at a victory celebration in one of the palace's halls. He sends word to the singer that he wishes to speak with her after the performance. Spoletta enters with the message that no trace of Angelotti has been found, but that Cavaradossi has been arrested and brought to the palace. The painter denies any knowledge of the fugitive's whereabouts. Tosca appears and Cavaradossi whispers to her to betray nothing. She answers negatively when Scarpia asks her if she has ever met Angelotti's sister, the Countess Attavanti.

Cries of pain are heard from the next room. Tosca realizes that Cavaradossi is being tortured. His moans break her resistance, and she gives away Angelotti's hiding place: he is in the well in the garden of Cavaradossi's house. Blood streaming from his wounds, Cavaradossi is dragged to a sofa in Scarpia's room.

A messenger comes in to inform the police chief that Napoleon—not the Italian army as previously thought—has been victorious. Hearing this, Cavaradossi gives vent to a spirited hymn of praise for freedom from tyranny. Overcome with rage, Scarpia commands that the painter be executed the following morning. Tosca is restrained as Cavaradossi is led off. She tries to bribe Scarpia with money. He replies that there is only one price for her lover's rescue—Tosca herself. Stunned, she indicates acceptance of the conditions. Scarpia orders that Cavaradossi's punishment be a mock execution. Tosca also demands that Scarpia sign papers assuring safe passage from Rome for her and Cavaradossi. When Scarpia gets up from his desk, he is confronted by Tosca who has picked up a knife from the dinner table. She plunges the blade into his breast, and retrieves the travel papers from the dying man's hand. She takes two candlesticks from the table, places them near Scarpia's head, and lays a crucifix on his chest. Unobserved, she slips away.

Act III. It is dawn. Atop the Castel Sant' Angelo preparations are being made for the shooting of Cavaradossi. He is led on and the final formalities begin. Cavaradossi begs the officer in charge for permission to write a few words of farewell to Tosca. Tosca appears, and Spoletta and the guards retire to give the lovers their last minutes of privacy. Tosca whispers to Cavaradossi that she has obtained his freedom and is in possession of travel papers. The firing squad will use blanks, not bullets, and Cavaradossi is to fall down as if dead. Tosca warns him not to get up again until she assures him that it is safe. Believing that no execution will take place, Cavaradossi refuses to have his eyes blindfolded. The firing squad shoots and he crumbles to the ground. The soldiers exit. When Tosca tells Cavaradossi to rise, she is horrified to discover that her lover is dead. At that moment, Spoletta comes back. He has found Scarpia's body and is about to arrest Tosca. With all her strength, she pushes him away and throws herself over the ramparts of the castle.

Tosca (Leontyne Price) gives vent to her hatred for Scarpia (Josh Wheeler) when she is summoned to the private study of the demanding police chief. NBC TV Opera production.

LA

TRAVIATA

LA TRAVIATA

In the play *La Dame aux Camélias,* by Alexander Dumas the younger, Giuseppe Verdi (1813-1901) thought he had found an effective literary basis for a new opera. The play represented to him the fulfillment of his longing for "new, great, beautiful subjects." The opera, entitled *La Traviata* (The Strayed One), had a cool reception at its Venice première. "*Traviata* yesterday was a fiasco. Is it my fault or the singers'? . . . Time will tell," wrote Verdi.

Traviata was created approximately the same time as *Il Trovatore.* In the dramatic intensity of its atmosphere, however, and in its musical characterizations, the opera towers above *Il Trovatore.* The spirited party scenes in the first and third acts, from which emerge great ensembles, are masterpieces of dramatic contrast. The preludes to Acts I and IV effectively set the mood for the action.

• • •

Opera in 4 acts. Libretto by Francesco Maria Piave, based on the play *La Dame aux Camélias* by Alexander Dumas, *fils. Première:* Teatro la Fenice, Venice, 1853.

Characters: Violetta Valery, courtesan (soprano); Alfredo Germont, her lover (tenor); Giorgio Germont, his father (baritone); Flora Bervoix, Violetta's friend (mezzo-soprano); Gastone, Viscount of Létorières (tenor); Baron Douphol (baritone); Marquis d'Obigny (bass); Dr. Grenvil (bass); Annina, Violetta's companion (mezzo-soprano); ladies, gentlemen, servants.

Locale: In and near Paris. *Time:* About 1840.

• • •

Act I. A gay party is taking place at the home of Violetta, a well-known figure of the Paris *demi-monde.* Among the guests is Alfredo Germont, who falls passionately in love with Violetta upon meeting her. They drink a toast, and the guests join in the refrain. After Violetta has a fainting spell, Alfredo learns that her health is poor. He proclaims his love for her, and Violetta, who has known love only for pleasure and material things, is moved by the purity and strength of his feeling. As the guests depart she gives Alfredo a camelia; she says he may see her again when the flower wilts. When she is alone she muses over the new emotions that have so suddenly stirred her; however, she doubts that she could ever give up her pleasure-seeking existence. Not even Alfredo's renewed declaration of love coming from the garden below can change her attitude; she decides she must forget him.

Renata Tebaldi as the beautiful Violetta. Metropolitan Opera.

Act II. Alfredo has persuaded Violetta to move with him to a home in the country outside Paris. There she lives an idyllic life devoted wholly to her new love. When Alfredo learns that Violetta has sold her belongings to support him, he rushes off to Paris to get more money. Unexpectedly, Alfredo's father visits Violetta and accuses her of ruining his son. He informs her that Alfredo's bad reputation is endangering the betrothal of Alfredo's sister. He then begs her to give up Alfredo. Deeply moved, Violetta decides to sacrifice her love and return to her previous life. Before leaving she writes a few lines to Alfredo. When Alfredo finds the message upon his return, he is distraught. On the writing table he discovers a letter inviting Violetta to a party at Flora's villa that very night. He suspects his rival Baron Douphol of persuading Violetta to betray him. Tortured by jealousy and suspicion, he decides to attend the party himself. His father returns and tries to calm Alfredo's agitation.

Act III. A masked ball is taking place at Flora's luxurious home. Alfredo mingles among the guests and participates in the gambling. When Violetta appears on the arm of her admirer Douphol, Alfredo makes insulting remarks. A call to the gambling table interrupts the clash about to develop between the two men. Alfredo soon returns to the room, followed by Violetta. She begs him, in vain, to leave the house. Alfredo insists she come with him and, frantic with despair, she says she loves the Baron. Alfredo curses Violetta in the presence of the assembled guests. He throws at her feet the money he has won from Douphol. It is payment for her services, he explains. Violetta tries to assure Alfredo of her love and, overcome with excitement, collapses. Alfredo is remorseful. He is led away by his father.

Act IV. Violetta is broken in body and spirit. Her rich admirers have forsaken her and, accompanied only by Annina, she awaits death in her modest new quarters. The doctor gives her only a few hours to live. As she lies near death, she rereads a letter from the elder Germont informing her that the Baron was wounded in the duel and that Alfredo has gone abroad. Alfredo appears and for a moment Violetta regains vitality. Once again Alfredo and Violetta declare their eternal love and make plans to begin life anew far away from Paris. As she tries to rise, however, Violetta realizes that the end is near. She gives him a medallion, saying that she wants the pure young girl he will one day marry to have it. The doctor returns, this time accompanied by Alfredo's father. Suddenly Violetta senses the presence of death. She sinks into Alfredo's arms.

Maria Callas as Violetta at La Scala, Milan, in the early 1950's.

TRISTAN

und isolde

TRISTAN UND ISOLDE

Richard Wagner (1813-1883) made use of the first years of his exile from Germany to write numerous literary works. He felt the necessity of giving an account of the conditions under which art could flourish in that critical time. The result, besides lesser writings, was the lengthy manuscripts of *Art and Revolution, The Art of the Future,* and *Opera and Drama.* He also returned to musical creation with the poem, *The Ring of the Nibelungen.* The theme of the old legend of Tristan and Isolde had already occupied his thoughts intensively in 1854, and in 1857, the tragic story of the two lovers so overwhelmed him that he decided to interrupt his work on the score of *Siegfried.*

The composer wrote each of the three acts of *Tristan und Isolde* in only a few months. The work was completely orchestrated by August, 1859. The basis for this sudden change of goal in his work lay in a deeply spiritual relationship between Wagner and Mathilde Wesendonck. Her husband, Otto Wesendonck, was a wealthy wholesale silk merchant who owned a palatial villa near Zurich. Both Wesendoncks were great lovers of art, and he offered the homeless composer and his wife Minna a guest house close by the main house. The result of a violent love between Wagner and Mathilde was the final break-up of the composer's marriage and the surrender of the little villa. The events of this painful period generated a high tension in Wagner that led to one of the greatest works in operatic literature.

Wagner used the epic by Gottfried von Strassburg as the main source for the poem. Thanks to his own poetic instincts, Wagner was able to make a far-reaching revision of the original. "With full confidence," he said, "I submerged myself more and more in the depths of the interior processes of the soul and fearlessly built from this most intimate center the world of external form." The conception of "endless melody," the utilization of chromatics, and the spiritualization of erotic emotions have not found such realization in any other work of Wagner's. "I have the feeling," he declared, "that I have ushered in something very significant with it; in any case, this work is more truly music than anything that I have previously written!"

•   •   •

Opera in 3 acts. Première: Court and National Theater, Munich, 1865.

Characters: Tristan (tenor); King Marke (bass); Isolde

(soprano); Kurvenal (baritone); Brangäne (mezzo-soprano); Melot, courtier (tenor or baritone); shepherd (tenor); steersman (baritone); sailor's voice (tenor).

Locale: Tristan's ship at sea, Marke's castle in Cornwall, Tristan's castle in Brittany. *Time:* Middle Ages.

•   •   •

Act I. Isolde is being brought from Ireland to Cornwall by Tristan, who is at the helm of the ship, to marry his uncle, King Marke. The King has heard of the beauty of the young princess and ardently seeks her hand. Earlier, Tristan himself had fought and killed Morold, Isolde's betrothed, who had oppressed the people of Cornwall. Afterward, under the name of Tantris, he had come to Ireland and been cured of his wounds by Isolde, skilled in medicinal herbs. She had recognized him by a nick in his sword, for she had found the missing piece in the head of the dead Morold. To be revenged, she had wanted then to kill Tristan, but he had looked in her eyes and an inexplicable power prevented her. Now, yielding to the demands of her parents, she declared herself ready to marry Marke in order to put an end to the wars between Ireland and Cornwall.

In a state of emotional turmoil, she entreats Tristan through Brangäne to come to her. She desires expiation and redemption in a common death with him. His comrade-in-arms, Kurvenal, mocks Isolde by describing Tristan's victory over Morold. Hate and vindictiveness sprout simultaneously in Isolde.

Brangäne hopes to be able to kindle Isolde's love for King Marke through her knowledge of magic potions. Isolde, on the other hand, wants to hear only of the death potion, which Brangäne also possesses. Tristan recognizes Isolde's true feelings behind her hate-filled words and is ready to partake of the cup of reconciliation with her, though he feels a dark premonition. Brangäne, however, has secretly mixed a love potion instead of the poison Isolde had asked for. Tristan and Isolde empty the cup and are seized by a love that overcomes all restraint. Scarcely aware of anything but themselves, they sink into each other's arms, while the ship nears the coast amidst the bustling and singing of the crew. After the first transport of love, Tristan, tormented by gloomy forebodings, exclaims: "O bliss full of knavery! O happiness, consecrated by deception!"

Act II. At daybreak, Marke and his entourage leave

for the hunt. Isolde waits for her beloved. The extinguishing of the torch by the castle door was to be the signal that he could make his appearance unnoticed. Brangäne warns Isolde about Melot, in whom she sees a dangerous enemy. While Brangäne goes up to the tower of the castle, Isolde signals by waving a scarf. Tristan appears and embraces his beloved. Completely carried away, they sing of their love. They believe that only in common death will they find the climax of their unrestrained surrender. Brangäne, who has already tried to warn them, breaks out with the resounding cry: "Tristan, save yourself!"

Led by Melot, King Marke appears with his hunting party. He is deeply shocked that Tristan, whom he considered the "truest of the true," should betray him. Tristan is not able to answer Marke's accusation. Tristan asks Isolde whether she will follow him wherever he may go. Isolde consents with her whole heart. Melot wants to avenge the shame inflicted on Marke and draws his sword. Tristan is badly wounded in the duel. Marke restrains Melot, however, from killing Tristan.

Act III. Tristan has been brought to his ancestral castle, Kareol, in Brittany, by Kurvenal, who hopes that the seriously wounded Tristan can be saved from death. While Tristan lies, as if lifeless, under a linden tree, a shepherd plays a melancholy tune. Kurvenal asks the shepherd to play a gay melody if he sights a ship. Tristan is

Tristan (Wolfgang Windgassen) lies wounded amid the ruins of his ancestral castle in Brittany, guarded by his faithful

awakened by the sound of the pipe, and asks longingly for Isolde. Kurvenal says that he has sent for her, since he hopes that once again her healing arts will help Tristan to recover. When the sad tune of the shepherd tells that no ship is in sight, Tristan deplores the dreadful love potion that has led to all his misfortune. In his feverish state, he imagines that he sees his beloved approaching.

Suddenly a joyful melody is heard on the pipe. Tristan has no doubt that Isolde is on the ship that has been sighted, and Kurvenal hurries out to receive her. Overcome by happiness, Tristan jumps up from his couch and tears the bandages from his wounds. Ecstatically he sinks in Isolde's arms. He dies with her name on his lips. Isolde kneels by him, and falls fainting at his side. The shepherd's playing again tells of an approaching ship—this time King Marke's. Melot appears and tries to attack Kurvenal with his sword, but instead, he himself is cut down by a sword blow. King Marke advances with his men. Kurvenal is defeated by the superior force and is slain. Marke, who had been informed by Brangäne about the unfortunate love potion, had generously wished to renounce Isolde and unite the lovers, but he sees sadly that it is too late. Isolde gazes on her beloved as though possessed. Her farewell song is also her final greeting to life. Transfigured, she expires on Tristan's body.

henchman Kurvenal (Gustav Neidlinger). Tristan awaits the ship that bears Isolde. Florence May Festival production, 1959.

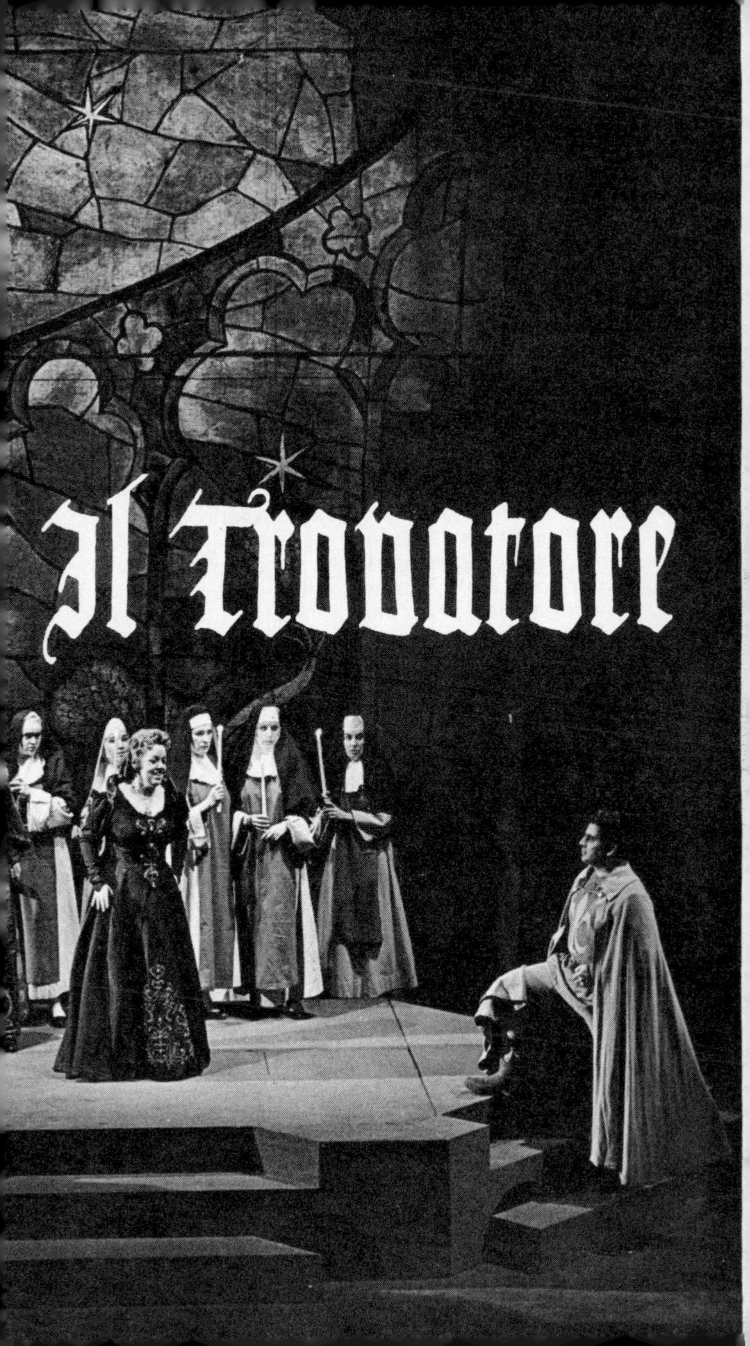
Il Trovatore

IL TROVATORE

Il Trovatore was once probably the most popular of Giuseppe Verdi's (1813-1901) operas, but it gradually has been overshadowed by a number of his other works. Without belittling the worth of *Il Trovatore,* it can be said that this change in taste has artistic justification. Even within the perspective of the average Italian opera text, *Il Trovatore*'s libretto cannot be counted among the best in Verdi's operas, but the music goes far in counterbalancing the implausibilities of the plot. The long-standing popularity of the work is best explained by the parts of Manrico and Leonora, which appeal to all *bel canto* singers, and by the highly dramatic characterization of Azucena.

• • •

Opera in 4 acts. Libretto by Salvatore Cammerano and Leone Emanuele Bardare, based on a play by Antonio Garcia Gutierrez. *Première:* Teatro Apollo, Rome, 1853.

Characters: Count di Luna (baritone); Leonora, Countess of Sargasto (soprano); Azucena, gypsy (mezzo-soprano or contralto); Manrico, officer in the Prince of Biscay's army (tenor); Ferrando, captain of the guard (bass); Inez, Leonora's confidante (soprano); Ruiz, lieutenant to Manrico (tenor); gypsies, soldiers, nuns, attendants.

Locale: Aragon and Biscay in Spain. *Time:* Fifteenth century.

• • •

Act 1, scene 1. In a hall of the Count di Luna's castle, Ferrando tells the guards a story about the Di Luna family's grim history. He tells of two sons, the younger of whom was bewitched and abducted by an old gypsy woman. She paid for the crime by being burned at the stake, but before dying she made her daughter Azucena swear to avenge her. Soon thereafter, the charred body of a child was found; it was unidentifiable, but was assumed to be that of the missing boy. The old Count, however, was not convinced, and on his death bed he passed on to his other son the mission of finding his lost brother.

Scene 2. In a park at night, the Countess Leonora tells her confidante Inez that she loves the troubadour Manrico. The Count di Luna, who wants Leonora for himself, has followed the women into the park. He overhears Manrico serenading Leonora. Leonora, mistaking the Count for Manrico in the dark, declares that she returns his love. When the troubadour appears and sees the Count, he raises the visor of his helmet. Di Luna recognizes him as an officer in the enemy's army, and they draw swords. Leonora tries to separate them. The men rush off to duel alone.

Act II, scene 1. Manrico has been wounded in the battle between the troops of Aragon and Biscay, and now rests in the gypsy camp, where Azucena, who has raised him from childhood, has been caring for him. Here in the mountains of Biscay, while the men sing their anvil chorus, Azucena tells Manrico of the horror of her mother's death by burning. Momentarily losing her senses, Azucena had thrown into the flames not the son of the Count, but her own child. Thus Manrico is led to suspect that he is not Azucena's son. A messenger arrives to tell him that Leonora, believing Manrico to have been killed in the duel with Di Luna, is about to enter a convent.

Scene 2. The Count comes to the convent to dissuade Leonora from taking the vow; he plans to abduct her. Manrico and his men arrive and prevent the abduction. Leonora flees with Manrico.

Act III, scene 1. Count di Luna and his army have occupied Castelor, an area under Manrico's command. Leonora has accompanied Manrico. Azucena, who has followed them, is taken prisoner. Di Luna learns that she is the gypsy woman who had supposedly thrown his brother into the flames, and he orders that she be burned at the stake.

Scene 2. At the castle, Manrico is told that Azucena has been condemned to death. He and Leonora were about to take their marriage vows in the chapel of the fortress; instead, he plans an immediate attack to save Azucena.

Act IV, scene 1. The Count's forces have overpowered Manrico, and he is imprisoned, together with Azucena. Led by Ruiz, Leonora manages to approach the dungeon. She hears Manrico's voice, and realizes when she hears the priests intone a "Miserere" that he awaits execution. Di Luna appears, and Leonora begs him to spare Manrico, but he refuses. Finally she offers to give herself to Di Luna if he will nullify the death penalty. He agrees.

Scene 2. In his cell, Manrico is told by Leonora of his pardon. But she pays for his freedom with her own life by taking poison from a ring on her finger. Di Luna orders Manrico's immediate execution. He drags Azucena to the window, so she can witness Manrico's death. "He was your brother!" she cries. "You are avenged, O mother!" And she falls lifeless to the ground.

WOZZECK

WOZZECK

It is unlikely that the history of opera offers another example in which a composer selected as his subject a dramatic fragment. When Alban Berg (1885-1935) saw a performance in Vienna of the tragedy *Woyzeck,* which had been pieced together from sketches by Georg Büchner, he was so fascinated by the power of the short and often merely symbolic scenes that he resolved to set them to music. Tragic circumstances had prevented the completion of the drama. Büchner, a highly gifted writer, died of typhus in 1837 at the age of twenty-three. His radical political views had forced him to flee from Germany, and he lived in Switzerland, where he taught natural sciences at the University of Zurich. He left behind a drama, *Danton's Death,* a comedy, *Leonce und Lena,* and the sketches for *Woyzeck.*

The subject of Büchner's *Woyzeck* was publicly executed for having murdered his girl friend in a fit of jealousy. Even though in Büchner's time psychoanalysis and psychotherapy had not found their way into the field of criminology, doctors made an intensive study to determine whether Wozzeck was a mentally deficient person who could not be held fully responsible for his actions. Büchner's deep sympathy here is with the soldier Wozzeck, the defenseless "underdog" who is crushed by fate. In the fragment and in the opera, Wozzeck dies by drowning, whether intentionally or accidentally is left open. The composer felt that Marie, who follows her sensual impulses, the vain, loud-mouthed drum major, the ridiculous figure of the doctor who fancies himself a great scientist, the captain moralizing in trite phrases, were all persons who in their basic characteristics were timeless. Thus the action of the play was well suited to Berg's complex, sensitive musical language, in spite of the apparent contrast between word and sound.

The unusual feature of this contemporary score is the use of old forms within an atonal harmonic framework. Although divested of their original character, suite, pavan, gigue, gavotte, air, passacaglia (with 24 variations), sonata, and rondo all find a place in the orchestral structure. However, the listener is hardly aware of the technical treatment of these traditional forms. The exciting atmosphere created by Berg's strong personal note, and by the poetry, casts a peculiar spell over the audience. It is primarily this characteristic which explains the growing success of *Wozzeck.* At present this work is one of the most frequently performed modern operas.

•   •   •

Opera in 3 acts, after the dramatic fragment by Georg Büchner. *Première:* Berlin State Opera, 1925.

Characters: Wozzeck, soldier (baritone); Drum Major (tenor); Andres, soldier (tenor); Captain (tenor); Doctor (bass); Marie (soprano); Margret (mezzo-soprano); Young Workmen (tenor and bass); The Fool (tenor); Soldier (tenor); Marie's son (child's voice).

Locale: A small German garrison town. *Time:* About 1820.

•   •   •

Act I, scene 1. Wozzeck shaves his captain. The latter cautions him not to brood too much over the problems of life. Wozzeck's thoughts are concerned with poor people, who are always victims of oppression. He defends himself against the captain's reproach about his and Marie's illegitimate child by arguing that even a poor man has a right to some happiness in life. But Wozzeck is worried about his beloved Marie and their child, for whom it is so difficult to provide. He is also afraid that Marie will be lured away by some of her many admirers.

Scene 2. Wozzeck and his comrade Andres are cutting reeds outside the town gates. The blood-red sunset produces in Wozzeck forebodings of disaster.

Scene 3. From the window of her little house Marie sees the passing military band whose drum major greets her with an air of familiarity. She sings her little boy to sleep. Wozzeck appears, strangely disturbed, and Marie tries to calm him.

Scene 4. For a pittance, Wozzeck permits the doctor to use him for his pseudo-scientific experiments. When Wozzeck tells of his dark forebodings, the charlatan is happy to find the subject of his experiments obsessed by an *idée fixe.*

Scene 5. In the evening the drum major and Marie meet in front of her house. He embraces her with brutal sensuality, and they enter the house together.

Act II, scene 1. Wozzeck notices the earrings given Marie by the drum major. She claims to have found them. As usual, he hands her his pay, and she becomes remorseful about her bad behavior.

Scene 2. The captain and the doctor meet Wozzeck. They pass sarcastic remarks about Marie's relations with the drum major, and Wozzeck runs off furiously.

Scene 3. On the street he confronts Marie. Hesitatingly, she admits her infidelity. He wants to hit her, but she cries that she would rather be stabbed with a knife than chastised. Wozzeck is completely bewildered and keeps repeating her phrase—"rather a knife . . ."

Scene 4. In a beer garden Marie is dancing with the drum·major. Wozzeck hears her merry laughter and goes into a wild rage. But the dance is stopped, a soldier begins a drunken song, and someone else delivers a sermon. A fool begins talking to Wozzeck, and as Wozzeck sits listening, he seems to weaken more.

Scene 5. In the barracks, while his comrades are sleeping in their bunks, Wozzeck broods over his fate. The drum major comes in and brags about his new conquest. Half drunk, he offers Wozzeck his bottle of schnapps. Wozzeck looks the other way with contempt and starts to whistle. A fight ensues between the two and Wozzeck is beaten. Triumphantly, the drum major leaves the room. Wozzeck rises and stares silently in front of him.

Act III, scene 1. By candlelight Marie reads the Biblical story of Christ and the adulteress. She begs the Saviour to have mercy on her too.

Scene 2. Wozzeck and Marie are walking on a forest path to a nearby pond. Marie senses approaching disaster and tries to escape, but Wozzeck falls upon her and plunges a knife into her breast.

Scene 3. At a dance in the tavern, Marie's neighbor, Margret, sees blood on Wozzeck's hand. He claims to have cut himself and leaves quickly. Everyone crowds around to see the blood, but Wozzeck runs out as fast as he can.

Scene 4. Wozzeck fears to be identified as the murderer, and he flings the knife he had left at the scene of the crime into the pond. Afraid the water is not deep enough where the knife fell, he wades into the pond and drowns. The captain and doctor pass by and hear a gurgling sound. Both flee the "haunted" spot.

Scene 5. The next day, Marie's little son is playing outside the house with the other small children in the street and appears to be as happy as usual. Then some older children come toward them and announce that the dead body of the child's mother has been found, but he is too young to understand them. When all of the children leave to learn more about the gruesome tragedy, Marie's son continues to play and sing to himself. But suddenly he notices that he is alone, and he toddles off after the others.

ght in the barracks. Production of the Compagnie Rafael
guez Vigouroux at Theater du Vieux Colombier, Paris.

PICTURE CREDITS

6-7 Metropolitan Opera Assn. / 8-9 Sedge LeBlang, Metropolitan Opera Assn. / 10-11 Irifoto / 12-13 NBC TV, NBC Opera / 16 Sedge LeBlang, Metropolitan Opera Assn. / 17 Metropolitan Opera Assn. / 18-19 Almberg Preinitz, Royal Opera, Stockholm / 22 NBC TV / 23 NBC TV / 24-25 Metropolitan Opera Assn. / 28-29 Metropolitan Opera Assn. / 31 NBC TV / 32-33 Metropolitan Opera Assn. / 34 Opera News / 35 Sedge LeBlang, Metropolitan Opera Assn. / 36 Sedge LeBlang, Metropolitan Opera Assn. / 38-39 NBC TV, NBC Opera / 41 Erio Piccagliani / 44 Paramount Pictures, International Telemeter Co. Production / 45 New York City Opera / 47 Paramount Pictures, International Telemeter Co. Production / 48-49 Sedge LeBlang, Metropolitan Opera Assn. / 52-53 NBC TV / 54-55 Salzburger Festspiele Presseburo, Salzburg Festival / 58 Franz Hausmann, Austrian Information Service / 60-61 Jurgen Simon, Komische Oper of East Berlin / 65 Jurgen Simon / 66-67 Sedge LeBlang, Metropolitan Opera Assn. / 69 Sedge LeBlang, Metropolitan Opera Assn., Opera News / 70-71 Cosmo-Sileo Associates, New York City Opera / 73 Metropolitan Opera Assn. / 74-75 Franz Hausmann, Austrian Information Service, Vienna State Opera / 76-77 Gunter Englert, Frankfurt am Main / 79 Vienna State Opera Production / 80-81 Festspiele Bayreuth / 85 Festspiele Bayreuth / 86-87 Frank Lerner, Metropolitan Opera Assn. / 88-89 Skelton Studios / 90 London Records / 92-93 Indiana University / 95 NBC TV / 97 Metropolitan Opera Assn. / 98-99 Salzburger Festspiele Presseburo, Salzburg Festival / 102 Salzburger Festspiele Presseburo / 104-105 Salzburger Festspiele Presseburo, Salzburg Festival / 109 Ellinger / 110-111 Maria

Austria / 112-113 Rudolf Betz, Opera News, Bavarian State Opera / 115 Sedge LeBlang, Metropolitan Opera Assn. / 119 German Tourist Office / 120-121 Erio Piccagliani, Opera News, La Scala / 122-123 Barry Glass, Vancouver Opera Assn. / 125 Barry Glass, Vancouver Opera Assn. / 126-127 Ellinger, Opera News, Salzburg Festival / 131 Metropolitan Opera Assn. / 132-133 NBC TV, NBC Opera / 135 Gunter Englert, Frankfurt am Main / 136 Louis Melancon, Metropolitan Opera Assn. / 138-139 Vandamm, New York Theater Guild Production / 141 Vandamm / 142-143 Alix Jeffry / 144-145 Louise Pote, Colorado Central City Opera / 148 Metropolitan Opera Archives / 150-151 Sedge LeBlang, Metropolitan Opera Assn. / 154-155 German Information Center, Bayreuth Festival / 158-159 German Information Center, Bayreuth Festival / 162-163 German Information Center, Bayreuth Festival / 166-167 German Tourist Information Office / 168-169 German Information Center, Bayreuth Festival / 173 Eugene Cook / 174-175 Fred Fehl, New York City Opera / 179 Eugene Cook / 180-181 NBC TV, NBC Opera / 182-183 NBC TV / 185 NBC TV / 186-187 Rudolf Betz, Bayreuth Festival / 190-191 German Tourist Information Office / 192-193 Gunter Englert, Frankfurt am Main, Frankfurt Municipal Opera / 197 NBC TV / 198-199 Gunter Englert, Frankfurt am Main, Frankfurt Municipal Opera / 201 Louis Melancon, Metropolitan Opera Assn. / 203 Erio Piccagliani / 204-205 Foto Barzacchi, Rome Opera / 208-209 Foto Marchiori, Opera News / 210-211 Sedge LeBlang, New York City Opera / 214-215 Angus McBean, Opera News, Covent Garden / 219 Erich Essing, Magnum Photos. / Several photographs have appeared in *Musical America*.

SIGNET CLASSICS

The Signet Classics
Shakespeare Series:

The Histories

extensively revised and updated expert commentary
provides more enjoyment through a greater
understanding of the texts

Available wherever books are sold or at
signetclassics.com

P.O. 0003357817